48 Monologues for TEENS

and how to master them

by JON EMM

The actor must use his imagination to be able to answer all questions (when, where, why, how). Make the make-believer existence more definite.

— Constantin Stanislavski

©2018 Jon Emm

ISBN-13:
9781719509893 (Jon Emm)
ISBN-10:
1719509891

Contents

Contents continues >

Contents (continued)

DRAMATIC

■ BOY OR GIRL

■ GIRL

■ BOY

Dedicated to the Teenager

So many things in your body are changing right now. That is not a judgement from an adult, but rather a biological fact. Perhaps you are overly emotional, frustrated, or defiant? Maybe you feel insecure, uncomfortable, awkward? Maybe you are lonely and angry and you think something is wrong with you? Or perhaps everything feels perfect as it is right now.

When you are a teenager it is hard to imagine what comes next or that the feelings you are experiencing now will ever change. You think that best friend of yours will be your best friend forever. Maybe. You think that you will never be better than that one classmate at anything. And that you will never like cottage cheese. You believe that this is who you are and who you will always be and you are totally certain that no adult could possibly understand.

What we do understand is that you are not stuck with what you've got. You will grow physically and emotionally and you will see the playing-field change dramatically. Some changes will be for the good, some maybe not as good. But it will change.

I wrote these monologues for the person you are *right now*. I am asking you to embrace who you are and plug-in so that you can express yourself fully and truthfully and move people with the beautiful power you possess right now, as a teenager. Enjoy the ride.

Introduction

T he monologue. It is defined in different ways, but each definition says that it is a speech of some sort, said *to* someone else. It is usually spoken by a character within a script, either a TV show, a movie, or a play. You may ask, how then can you use a monologue from a monologue book when there is no play or show or movie to support it? That is an excellent question. You are more than welcome to go and find a monologue from a play or movie or show. But be warned; that can be a challenge. Finding the right monologue is time consuming because there are thousands of plays and movie scripts published. You need to find one that is the right length, proper in its context, and close to your age. You will need to read the entire script as well to get the background for the character because it is possible the casting person or director knows the character already. And, you want to be relatively original, meaning you don't want to do the same monologue that every other teen is doing.

So I present to you the perfect compromise. In your hand is a book of original, active monologues, both comedic and dramatic. They are written for teenagers, they are all one minute in length, and each monologue is accompanied by a series of questions. The questions are there to make you think more deeply about the life of your character. As there is no script beyond the monologue, you must create one for yourself. You put your imagination to work and you develop a character made up of elements within your creative mind. The result will be a rich, endearing character with depth and honesty. Answer the questions and your character will possess not only a past, but a memory to access it. And your creation will be as unique as your fingerprint.

It is up to you whether or not you trust this process. Konstantin Stanislavski, the great director, teacher, and co-founder of the famous Moscow Arts Theatre, said that you do the work beforehand, then leave it alone when you go into performance. This means you answer all the questions around your character and thoroughly build the life of the character based on what you have garnered from the script (in this case, the monologue.) Then, trust that you have done the work and go for it. The words will be your own, they will be much less intimidating, and they will be easier to memorize. Your character will be alive and inspired as your lines come to you fresh and new every single performance. *This is because you know who your character is and what your character wants.*

Lastly, I want to share a story. I had a thirteen-year-old actor in my class present a monologue. She did a nice job with it. Later she told me that she really didn't feel like the questions helped. I said okay and I thanked her for doing the work and for taking the time to answer the questions. Three weeks later I asked her to do the monologue again. "I haven't looked at it in weeks!" she exclaimed. I convinced her to try. She went to the front of the class, took about thirty seconds to gather herself, and performed the monologue brilliantly. In fact, she did it better than she did the first time we saw it. She was stunned and so was the class. She couldn't imagine how the words came to her again after three weeks. I explained that because she answered all the questions thoroughly, her mind was remembering an event, and not just words on a page. That is the reason for the questions. Take it or leave it.

Answering the Questions

You will find that each monologue has questions that follow. It is completely up to you whether or not you choose to put in the effort to answer them. But I will tell you this: A good director will know if you just memorized words and have nothing behind the words. It really is that simple. The questions are there to give your character depth. What does this mean?

Depth in a character means the character has a life that is apparent beyond the words that he or she is speaking. Let's say, for example, that your character says, "I don't want to." Simple enough. Anyone can deliver that sentence, right? But to give your character depth, let's ask the question, *why*? Why don't you want to? Maybe you don't want to because you are a spoiled brat and you have always gotten your way. Maybe it's because you have done whatever it is you don't want to do before and gotten hurt. Or maybe you have a deep secret and if you were to do what is being asked, your secret might be revealed. Knowing who you are and what you want is the basis for giving your character depth. Answering the questions may make the work a little harder, but it also makes you a much more interesting actor to watch. And, the hard work gets easier each time you do it.

Often the words of the monologue answer some of the questions for you. The monologue may tell you where you are, or who you are talking to, or what happened just before you began speaking. Sometimes the monologue will make clear what it is that you want. That is a big one — knowing what you want. It is your objective and it is what motivates you to speak the words you are speaking. You will find that some of the same questions appear after every monologue. I want to discuss those in-depth here so that you can refer back to this page anytime and remind yourself how to answer them.

1. Challenge

The challenge explains what the actor can expect and the degree of difficulty of the monologue. For example, if the monologue calls for you to speak very fast and you are someone who speaks slowly, or vice-versa, then this monologue is likely going to be a challenge for you. If a monologue requires you to get very angry, and you don't allow yourself to express anger, then you may be challenged by that monologue. Another monologue may be loaded with punctuation (ellipsis, commas, periods), signaling thought changes that may happen mid-sentence. That monologue may simply be above your current capability. I'm not telling you not to attempt it, I am only stating what is going to be challenging for the actor.

2. What is this monologue about?

Simply put, "What the heck is going on here?" You should be able to say aloud what the monologue is about. If you cannot, read it again until you can answer what the heck is going on. If you still cannot say it, move on to another monologue.

3. Where are you?

Sometimes this answer is given in the monologue. Other times, it is not. Make sure you know exactly where your character is standing, so that you can get grounded. If you are outside your school, know *exactly* where outside the school you are. In the back of the school? By the basketball court? In the parking lot? What do you see? What do you hear? Who else is around? You have to make it real so that you can make your audience see what you see.

4. Who are you talking to?

Again, sometimes this is given. A brother, a friend, your mother. So if you don't have a brother, should you pass on this monologue? Of course not. But don't guess about your brother either. Create him thoroughly. If you see him, we'll see him. Who you are talking to is very important. Understand that we talk to a sister differently than we talk to the police and we talk differently to the principal than we do our best friend.

5. What do you want? How are you going to get it?

This is also known as your objective and it can be the most difficult question to answer. Yet knowing what you want is the most important question of all. Understand this: We ALWAYS have an objective when we are speaking. ALWAYS. Just observe people talking and ask, "Why is he or she saying that right now?" Are they trying to impress someone? Are they protecting someone? Are they trying to gain someone's trust? Are they in love? Are they trying to convince someone of something? Even when it seems like someone is just talking on and on, they want something. *Always!*

6. Are there any more questions you can ask yourself?

You may find yourself getting very involved in your character's back story. That is good. You may think of more questions that are not listed. Feel free to write them down. Let your imagination go wild. Your character will appreciate it and so will your audience.

7. Write your character's autobiography.

The autobiography is so important that if I was to ask you to do just one thing in preparation, I would ask you to write an autobiography. The autobiography lets you illustrate, in writing, where your character comes from, how he or she thinks, and why they may think that way. It is your opportunity to give yourself a different family, a different house and/or a completely different set of friends. Change your school, your teachers, even the country you come from! You can change it all, but be specific and write it down.

8. The magic IF. What would you do if you were in the situation that your character is in?

This is when you see the difference between yourself and your character. By taking note of how you would behave in a situation, you can then see, based on the words of the monologue, how your character is different from you. If a behavior is similar to your own behavior, don't spend too much time working on that because that behavior is natural to you. But when a behavior is much different than how you would behave, you'll want to work more on that part.

 Just a minute

It is important to note that the monologue should be about one minute long. That is the author's intention. Time yourself. If you are within a few seconds, you've got the timing down. If you are off by a full ten seconds or more, you need to figure out where to speed up or slow down. If there is no time limit on your monologue presentation and you feel it should be much slower or faster, then feel free to do with it as you wish. But most auditions are one minute in length.

 Pencil it in

Lastly, write everything in pencil, with the idea that it may change. You are not permanently stuck with a choice you made. Perhaps you decide that your character is an only-child. Then, after working on the piece, you conclude that he or she probably has a sibling based on something they said. Changing something about your character is not only okay, it is expected. If you really care about the piece you are working on, it will evolve and change as you work with it. Rarely do we make decisions about a character that are completely correct the first time. As in your life, embrace change and make it work for you.

Notes & Thoughts

COMEDIC
Monologues

COMEDIC

The Mother Machine   Boy or Girl

My mother had coffee this morning. That may not seem like a big deal to you, but you need to understand. Wait. Do you know my mother? No, of course not. My mother is, like, a very well-oiled mother-machine. She isn't like normal ladies at all. You know, the ones that gently stir their kids out of bed, say good morning really sweetly and then calmly go about their day with their little apron on. That *is* normal, right? But my mom, no way! I bet my mother doesn't even have an apron. She is all business. She is, like, a mad woman! Sometimes I wish I had a tranquilizer gun to slow her down. But then she moves so fast I'd never be able to hit her! Plus my dad would be furious. I have never actually seen it, but I bet in the morning she opens her eyes, takes a deep breath, puts on a tiny jet pack under her clothes, and blasts off! It's insanity. And today someone gave her coffee. I heard her talking to someone downstairs and I could smell coffee. The next thing I know, BOOM! My door flies open, I am whisked into the shower and now I'm here! Do I still have shampoo in my hair?

CHALLENGE: To make sure you do not stay on the same note the whole time. You are excited so you will be fast and animated, but you have to slow down at certain times. Find the moments where you would soften and slow down. Be big and be animated. Just find your changes and have a ball!

1. What is this monologue about?
2. Where are you?
3. Who are you talking to?
4. What was your moment before (before you begin speaking this monologue)?
5. What do you want? How are you going to get it?
6. What else does your mother do that makes her a "mother-machine?" Be specific.
7. Fill in the blanks. What happened this morning from the time you woke up until now?
8. Does your mother work? What does she do with her days? Describe her.
9. Why does your mother have to wake you up like that? Are you at all responsible? Do you try to sleep in? Are you a morning person? What about the rest of the family?
10. What is your mother like at night? Is she asleep on the couch? Is she still going strong? Are you like her in any way?
11. Are there any more questions that you can ask yourself?
12 Write an autobiography for this character. Build your character a life.
13. Remember the magic "if." What would *you* do if you were in this situation?

✎ **WRITE OUT** all of your answers. Be specific. It will get you closer to the truth of the scene, and you will create a stronger character.

⧗ **TIME YOURSELF.** This monologue was written to be about one minute long.

My Future Kids   Boy or Girl

There is no way I will be able to finish all this homework. Not by tomorrow anyway. Not even by the end of the week probably. If Miss Vivian was right here with me, I couldn't finish all this. She could be sitting right here, right next to me. And I can hear her now. "You can do it. Just think about the future. Think about your family that will be so happy that you worked so hard as a child so you could get a good job and take care of them." Then she'll say, "People you don't even know yet are counting on you!" Seriously? That is supposed to make me work harder? It totally freaks me out is what it does. Who are these people that are counting on me? I'm a kid! I don't want anybody to count on me. I just want to play games and go to P.E. Mr. Connors counts on me to do well at dodgeball and kickball. That should be enough, don't you think? He counts on us to choose teams, decide what color we are going to be, and play. I just want to play! Don't you? I don't want anybody I don't know yet watching me and rooting for me. Are they watching right now? I mean, that just gives me the creeps.

CHALLENGE: To make sure you do not stay on the same note the whole time. You are excited, or frustrated, but you cannot stay on the same level of excitement the entire monologue. Find your moments where you slow down and bring your voice down. Then pick it back up again. Really make us believe that you are freaked out by the thought of your future children watching your every move. You also have to imitate Miss Vivian. Have fun!

1. What is this monologue about?
2. Where are you? Is this where you always do your homework?
3. Who are you talking to? There is a hint in there that tells you that you are talking to another kid.
4. What was your moment before?
5. What do you want? How are you going to get it?
6. Describe Miss Vivian. Use a lot of detail to describe her. Remember, you have to use her voice in the monologue. Is she really sweet? Is she stern? Make a good decision here.
7. Do you (not your character) like P.E.? Write out what you love and what you don't like about P.E. class.
8. Describe Mr. Connors. Use a lot of detail. We want to see that he is real to you.
9. Picture your future children watching you. How does that make you feel really?
10. What is your homework? Will you really not get it done or are you exaggerating?
11. Are there any more questions that you can ask yourself?
12. Write an autobiography for this character. Build your character a life.
13. Remember the magic "if." What would *you* do if you were in this situation?

✐ **WRITE OUT** all of your answers. Be specific. It will get you closer to the truth of the scene, and you will create a stronger character.

⧗ **TIME YOURSELF.** This monologue was written to be about one minute long.

COMEDIC

Distractions   Boy or Girl

What are they doing? I can feel the whole apartment shake. How are you ever supposed to get your work done? Wait, I saw Tommy Clement right before we came in. Is that the Clements right next door to you? They go to our church. I can hear them. There is like twenty kids in that family. There's Cassidy, who is in the same grade as my sister, so she is like seventeen. Then there is Junior. Who names their kid Junior? Junior is a sophomore. Maybe Junior is a junior? And Nell, and Draymond, and Noah. I think they are all in the same grade. How is that even possible? Wait, maybe Noah is a cousin? That would make sense because Noah doesn't look like the rest of them. Well he does, but he doesn't. That would be so awesome if Noah was over there. There is Connie, of course. And then there are like eight little ones whose names all start with a 'J'. It's like Mr. and Mrs. Clement just decided to start over. I wonder what it would be like to come from a family *that* big? (Listening) Maybe I should ask my parents to start over.

CHALLENGE: To not talk on one note the whole time. You *must* find places to slow down and places to speed up. If you do not, people will not be able to keep up with you. And, it will be boring. There are a lot of words. Have pictures in your mind for everyone you are talking about and we will see them too. During this monologue you discover that the idea of a large family sounds cool. We need to see that discovery happen. Slow down, think, and picture it. Have fun!

1. What is this monologue about?
2. Where are you? This is your environment (smell, feel, see, hear). Be very specific.
3. Who are you talking to? Describe the person.
4. What was your moment before? What happened just before you began speaking?
5. What do you want? How are you going to get it?
6. Why are you at this apartment? It seems relatively unfamiliar to you. Have a good story about why you are there.
7. You need to describe all the Clements. Even the parents. How many are there really?
8. How many people are in your family? Obviously you don't have many siblings, maybe none. This is an opportunity to create a family for yourself.
9. You say, "There is Connie, of course." So you must know Connie. How do you know Connie? Don't just answer, "She's in my grade." Be specific. Do you sit by her? What's she like?
10. Describe the sound coming from the neighbors. What does it sound like?
11. Are there any more questions that you can ask yourself?
12. Write an autobiography for this character. Build your character a life.
13. Remember the magic "if." What would *you* do if you were in this situation?

✐ **WRITE OUT** all of your answers. Be specific. It will get you closer to the truth of the scene, and you will create a stronger character.

⧗ **TIME YOURSELF.** This monologue was written to be about one minute long.

Nicki Minaj

Boy or Girl

My brother got a hamster yesterday. Not my brother Dominick. *Joe* got a hamster. Dominick actually has a brain and wouldn't get a hamster. So I'm in my room doing calc and he is just … making so much noise. Then after a while he just barges into my room and he has this hamster in an aquarium and this thing is terrified because Joe is such a spazz. He reaches in and grabs this poor thing and says, "You have to meet beautiful Nicki Minaj." He thinks it looks like Nicki Minaj. All these wood chips are falling on my desk and I told him 'no', that I don't even want to meet the real Nicki Manaj. So he takes this thing back to his room. Then I hear this squeaking. I go in his room and Joe's gone and this thing is running on one of those wheels, like, as fast as it can possibly run. And it actually does look like Nicki Manaj, by the way. And I'm thinking, I can totally relate. I would be running away from Joe, too. Now I'm rooting for it, but this poor thing ran all night long! I need to get some grease for that stupid wheel or I may never pass another test as long as I live.

CHALLENGE: Pacing. This character is a smart person. You take Calculus. Don't go too fast. This is a one minute monologue. Time yourself. If it is too slow for you, choose a different monologue. Slow should not be confused with boring. You are thoughtful. You choose your words carefully. A great test for you mumbling, fast talkers.

1. What is this monologue about?
2. Where are you? This is your environment (smell, feel, see, hear). Be very specific. When you look around, what do you see?
3. Who are you talking to?
4. What was your moment before? What happened just before you began speaking?
5. Describe Joe. How old is he? What else does he do that is annoying? Build a relationship between you and Joe.
6. Why don't you want to like this hamster? Are you really against the hamster or is it more about Joe?
7. Describe your bedroom. Describe where you are sitting when Joe comes in and where his room is. Where is the hamster in his room? *Have a clear picture of what it looks like.* Can you draw the floor plan of your house?
8. Describe Dominick. Describe the difference in your relationship with him as opposed to Joe.
9. Describe Nicki Minaj, both the animal and the singer. What part of this animal actually looks like the real Nicki Minaj?
10. What is Calculus? If you are not familiar with it, look at it. It may help you develop this character.
11. Are there any more questions that you can ask yourself?
12. Write an autobiography for this character. Build your character a life.
13. Remember the magic "if." What would *you* do if you were in this situation?

✒ **WRITE OUT** all of your answers. Be specific. It will get you closer to the truth of the scene, and you will create a stronger character.

⧗ **TIME YOURSELF.** This monologue was written to be about one minute long.

COMEDIC

Paul and Paul

Boy or Girl

You know my neighbor Paul? The guy with the white Pit Bull? He got married yesterday to a man. They came over last night and he introduced us to his husband. *His* name is Paul, too. Paul *also*, I should say. It's so weird because we didn't even know he was gay. My father said he thought Paul was probably gay, but my mom said my dad had no idea. My dad said he picked up on things a little bit. My mom was like, "What kind of things did you pick up on, Dirk?" I think my mom was a little bent out of shape because she was completely in the dark about Paul being gay. My dad said Paul mentioned going to Benson's once — that bar down by the pier. My mom told him that Benson's isn't even a gay bar, and my dad said that it *is* a gay bar on Wednesday nights. So of course my mom asked him how he would know Benson's was a gay bar on Wednesdays and my dad said he had seen the calendar for Benson's in the Weekly. My mother called him an idiot and said that doesn't mean anything. I don't think he knew either. None of us knew. The husband, Paul, seems pretty cool. And he has a Harley.

CHALLENGE: Pace. You are telling a story. Even though this only happened yesterday, it is still in the past. If you are not a good storyteller, this can be a tough piece. Be expressive, be animated, and tell a good tale. You are trying to make whoever is listening laugh, so go for it!

1. What is this monologue about?
2. Where are you? This is your environment (smell, feel, see, hear). Be very specific. When you look around, what do you see?
3. Who are you talking to? A friend? A relative? It is someone who has been to your house as he knows the guy with the Pit Bull? Who is it? Does it change for you if you say it to a girl? Or a boy?
4. What was your moment before? What happened just before you began speaking?
5. Describe Paul in great detail. Have a very clear picture in your head of who Paul is.
6. Where were you when Paul brought Paul over? Have a clear image. How did he introduce his husband? How did it make you feel when he told you?
7. Describe Paul's husband. Describe his Harley. What color is it?
8. Tell us about the pier where Benson's is. How far is it from your house?
9. Describe your parent's relationship. They seem to kid each other. Tell us about them. Do you have any siblings?
10. How do you, the actor, feel about gay marriage? Is it something you are totally fine with? How does the way you feel about gay marriage differ from the way this character feels about it?
11. Are there any more questions that you can ask yourself?
12. Write an autobiography for this character. Build your character a life.
13. Remember the magic "if." What would *you* do if you were in this situation?

✐ **WRITE OUT** all of your answers. Be specific. It will get you closer to the truth of the scene, and you will create a stronger character.

⌛ **TIME YOURSELF.** This monologue was written to be about one minute long.

Home Delivery — Boy or Girl

COMEDIC

We started getting our dinner delivered. Not like pizza or Chinese food. We actually have to make it once it gets to our house. My dad is deployed and mom works all the time so she decided we should do this. At first I was like, wait. We still have to cook everything? I said, "Mom, this is crazy! Why don't we just get pizza? It's ready to eat and I could eat pizza every day!" And she was like, "We'll get too fat and then your father won't even recognize us when he gets home!" I told her that he would recognize us. I mean, we're living in his house! Who would we be? So mom says cooking together will be good for us. And at first I was like, no! I can't. I don't want to. But then I saw everything that comes in the box. It's like a puzzle. You get the vegetables, the meat, the sauce, the potatoes, everything. It is so cool. Last night we made beef tips and mac and cheese! It was awesome! My mom and I make dinner three nights a week. I chop, I mince, I julienne. I didn't even know what that meant before. I love it. A big edible puzzle. That's what it's like. And it's so good!

CHALLENGE: You must convince us that you do not like the idea at first and eventually come around to loving it. When you have a large arc (going from one frame-of-mind to another) you have to make sure you bring your audience along with you each step of the way. It can be tricky. Make sure your speed (tempo) changes as you get more excited.

1. What is this monologue about?
2. Where are you? This is your environment (smell, feel, see, hear). Be very specific. When you look around, what do you see? What time of day is it?
3. Who are you talking to? Describe the person or persons.
4. What was your moment before? What happened just before you began speaking?
5. Describe your kitchen where you prepare the food.
6. Describe your front door and where the food gets delivered to. What does the box look like?
7. How do you feel when you open the box of food? Do you know anyone who has food delivered?
8. What kind of pizza do you like? Who delivers it to you?
9. Describe your mother completely. Talk about what it is like to prepare dinner with her.
10. Where is your father deployed to? Do research. Where are our soldiers going? How long until he comes home?
11. Are there any more questions that you can ask yourself?
12 Write an autobiography for this character. Build your character a life.
13. Remember the magic "if." What would you do if you were in this situation?

✎ **WRITE OUT** all of your answers. Be specific. It will get you closer to the truth of the scene, and you will create a stronger character.

⧖ **TIME YOURSELF.** This monologue was written to be about one minute long.

COMEDIC

The Man Upstairs

Boy or Girl

Our landlord told us the guy that lives above us is a little strange. She told us he was a tad insane, but that he keeps to himself. My mom said that was fine as long as he keeps to himself. So, I get up really early in the morning and I will say that he may be alone up there in his little apartment, but he sure isn't *alone* in his head! I hear him. At first I thought he had company. I was like, hey Walt has company. His name is Walt. But then I started hearing him talking to these people that definitely were not up there in his apartment. I heard him talking to a woman and I heard him say, "The president won't mind if you sleep over, Michelle." Honestly. I thought, the president? Then he said, "Fine. Tell Barrack I said 'hi' and that I'm sorry if I overstepped." He was talking to Michelle Obama! So then I started listening closely. I heard him talking to Kaitlin Jenner last week. He was asking her if she watched the decathlon. I heard him speaking to Simon Cowell about the way he treated someone on America's Got Talent. I heard him asking Flo about insurance. And he was talking to Adele just last night. I thought, who needs roommates? This guy has all the friends he needs.

CHALLENGE: To make sure you don't come off like you are making fun of someone with mental illness. You have to trust that the lines are funny as they are because if you try to enhance this piece, you will sound insensitive. Play it straight and don't go for the laugh. It will be much funnier that way.

1. What is this monologue about?
2. Where are you? This is your environment right now. (Smell, feel, see, hear). Be very specific. When you look around, what do you see?
3. Who are you talking to? A friend? A teacher? Try talking to different people. How does it change?
4. What was your moment before? What happened just before you began speaking?
5. Describe Walt. Be very specific. His size, his hair, his eyes. Do you like him? Have you ever spoken to him? Is he nice?
6. Describe your apartment. Where do you hear him speaking? Does his voice come through a vent? Are you listening from your bed or do you get up?
7. Describe moving into your apartment. Where did you move from?
8. Have you ever dealt with anyone with mental illness before? Who was it? Describe it.
9. Are there any more questions that you can ask yourself?
10. Write an autobiography for this character. Build your character a life.
11. Remember the magic "if." What would *you* do if you were in this situation?

✎ **WRITE OUT** all of your answers. Be specific. It will get you closer to the truth of the scene, and you will create a stronger character.

⧗ **TIME YOURSELF.** This monologue was written to be about one minute long.

Pool Rules

Boy or Girl

Rule number one, no dunking. If you dunk anybody, me in particular, consider yourself banned for life. I don't care if global warming turns the planet into an oven, you will not get back into this pool. That goes for pulling anybody under by their legs, too. Me in particular. Rule number two, no running around the pool. My little sister split her head open running past the diving board and ruined all the fun. It was totally gross and I ended up throwing up in the pool. So don't run. And don't puke in the pool. That's not an official rule, but it should be. And rule number three, no peeing in the pool. My father told me he got that stuff that turns the water red if you pee in the pool. I don't know if it's true or not, but whenever I get the urge I use the toilet in the pool house. I do not want to be the one that finds out my father was telling the truth. Please use the pool house to pee. Don't dunk, don't run, and don't pee. We're cool about everything else. Oh, and don't just show up with other people. I like to know who is coming so I can prepare properly. Plus, if I don't know them, I will feel funny about the rules and they might pee in the pool and then they would hate me forever for not telling them. Understand?

CHALLENGE: You are listing the rules. You don't want your monologue to sound like one big list. You need to change the inflection of your voice. Talk faster, slower, higher, lower. Just don't let is sound like a big list. You also have to make us see the images clearly.

1. What is this monologue about?
2. Where are you? This is your environment (smell, feel, see, hear). Be very specific. When you look around, what do you see? Are you by the pool?
3. Who are you talking to? Are you talking to a group or just one person? Try it both ways? Remember, whoever you are talking to has not heard the pool rules before.
4. What was your moment before? What happened just before you began speaking? Are you about to go swimming? Is something going on later?
5. We will get the impression you do not like to be dunked. Tell us why. Be descriptive.
6. Describe what happened when your sister cut her head open. Did you all have to go to the hospital?
7. Describe your sister. Her name, her age, her size. Does she have a scar on her head? Do you have any more siblings?
8. Where were you when your father told you he put the stuff in the water that makes your urine red? Be descriptive.
9. What do you mean when you say you like to know who is coming over so you can prepare properly? How do you prepare differently from one person to the next?
10. What games do you play in the pool? What kind of fun stuff do you have around there?
11. Are there any more questions that you can ask yourself?
12. Write an autobiography for this character. Build your character a life.
13. Remember the magic "if." What would you do if you were in this situation?

✐ **WRITE OUT** all of your answers. Be specific. It will get you closer to the truth of the scene, and you will create a stronger character.

⏳ **TIME YOURSELF.** This monologue was written to be about one minute long.

COMEDIC

Divorce Court   Boy or Girl

I love Divorce Court. I record it every single day and I watch it when I get home from school. It's the best show on TV. Know why? Because it's real. My parents never got a divorce okay, but if they did, I'd have a new father. Right? Or a new mother, depending on who is worse. Not that I want a new mother or father. But it would be so weird. And Judge Lynn Toller is so reasonable and wise. She always tells them if she thinks they can work it out or if they need to hit the highway. Sometimes, I'm like, there's no way, but the judge thinks they can manage. It's heart-warming. Unlike Paternity Court. Now that is just nasty. Neither of them is sure if it's their kid or not. Well mom, mom always knows it's hers, right? Unless there was a mix-up in the hospital. But dad, not so much. And he's hoping and crying. And sometimes the guy is hoping the kid *isn't* his because he can't stand mom or the kid. Then the results come in and mom is like, "I told you it wasn't yours! I told you!" And I'm like, you're proud right now? Seriously?

CHALLENGE: Speed. You are talking about your favorite show so you know exactly what you mean. But your audience may have never seen these shows before and they are hearing about them for the first time. You need to talk fast, as you are delivering a lot of information, but you must make it very clear what you are talking about. Time the piece to be one minute, then you'll know you have the intended speed.

1. What is this monologue about?
2. Where are you? This is your environment (smell, feel, see, hear). Be very specific. When you look around, what do you see?
3. Who are you talking to? A friend? A teacher? Remember, it is someone who doesn't know you really well or they would already know that you watch every day after school.
4. What was your moment before? What happened just before you began speaking? Perhaps someone said, "I told you my favorite show. What's yours?"
5. Where do you watch? On your computer? On TV? Where is your TV? Describe the room.
6. What else do you watch on TV?
7. Do you feel guilty watching TV? If you said yes, what else should you be doing after school?
8. Watch two episodes of Divorce Court and Paternity Court. What do you really think of these shows? Who do these shows try to appeal to? What do you like about them?
9. If your parents are divorced, describe what it was like before and after the divorce. If your parents are together, can you describe anyone else's situation?
10. Why is this monologue funny?
11. Are there any more questions that you can ask yourself?
12. Write an autobiography for this character. Build your character a life.
13. Remember the magic "if." What would *you* do if you were in this situation?

✐ **WRITE OUT** all of your answers. Be specific. It will get you closer to the truth of the scene, and you will create a stronger character.

⧗ **TIME YOURSELF.** This monologue was written to be about one minute long.

Unfriending

COMEDIC

Boy or Girl

I was thinking I'm just going to unfriend her. Don't call me a wuss! It's just that I can't stand making someone feel bad. I know you're gonna say that unfriending her is going to make her feel bad too, but not as bad as actually telling her to her face that I don't want her around. She is just so… You know what she did yesterday? She told Delonte that my birthday party was boring. First of all, *she's* the most boring person in the universe! I'm surprised she didn't bring her AP Physics homework with her to the party. Just thinking of her makes me… And secondly, I didn't invite Delonte and I told everybody not to mention it to him. *You* knew not to mention it to him. But no! She just shoots-off her mouth anyway. She's always doing that. And, she is always, always, always sharing stupid stuff to my timeline. That's it! I'm doing it. I'm unfriending her. (Pause) She's so… And if my mom didn't work with her mom, she wouldn't have known about the party either. Now Delonte's mad at me.

CHALLENGE: To be frustrated without totally whining through the whole monologue. Nobody likes a whiner. You must convince us that this girl is a jerk, and you are not. Find the right pace — slow down, speed up, and you will be funny. This one should be fun!

1 What is this monologue about?
2. Where are you? This is your environment (smell, feel, see, hear). Be very specific. When you look around, what do you see?
3. Who are you talking to? Remember, the person was at your birthday party.
4. What was your moment before? What happened just before you began speaking?
5. Describe this girl in detail. Have a very solid image of her in your mind.
6. What kind of stuff does she share on your timeline? What kind of stuff really bugs you?
7. Who is Delonte? Why wasn't he invited?
8. What was your birthday party like? How many people were invited? Who was there?
9. You say she is "always shooting her mouth off." Give me an example of another time she shot her mouth off.
10. You say "you can't stand making someone feel bad." Give an example of a time you made someone feel bad.
11. Are there any more questions that you can ask yourself?
12. Write an autobiography for this character. Build your character a life.
13. Remember the magic "if." What would *you* do if you were in this situation?

✎ **WRITE OUT** all of your answers. Be specific. It will get you closer to the truth of the scene, and you will create a stronger character.

⏳ **TIME YOURSELF.** This monologue was written to be about one minute long.

COMEDIC

Cheating   Boy or Girl

Please just explain to me what the big deal is? What harm is there to you? Wait, better yet, let me tell you why I think you *should* let me see your test before you tell me why you shouldn't. Okay, you are wicked smart. Everyone knows how ridiculously smart you are. You'll probably be our val... valor... valo... whatever that is. The smartest kid in our class. Who's smarter than you? Olivia? I don't think so. And you are cuter than her so if it comes down to a vote for who should get it, you'll win for sure. So, I copy your exam. *Not all of it.* Just a little to get me through the tough spots. I am really super good at glancing over and getting a bunch of answers at once so Ms. Walton will never catch me. I'm like, glance and memorize. I have a photographic memory. All I need is a quick peek and I've got all I need. In fact, you won't even know I'm doing it. That's what you can tell Ms. Walton if she catches me! We'll just say you didn't know. No one even has to know we had this conversation right now. (Looks around) Oh man! There aren't any cameras around here, are there?

CHALLENGE: Changing speeds. You are trying to make a case, but it is lame. You are thinking on your feet. You are trying to convince a smart person that your stupid idea is a good one. You need to be charming. You need to be convincing. And you need to not sound like a total idiot. You will need to change your timing as you come up with different reasons and ideas. Don't race through it at one speed. You won't be convincing. You need this person. Convince them. Tricky!

1. What is this monologue about?
2. Where are you? In the hallway at school? Cafeteria? Somewhere outside of school?
3. Who are you talking to? Describe this person with great detail. Try making the person a boy and also try it as a girl. How does it change it? Which do you prefer?
4. What was your moment before? What happened just before you said these words?
5. What do you want? How are you going to get it?
6. Let's assume you cheat. Who else do you cheat off? Describe the situations.
7. In what class is it that you want to cheat off this person? Describe the class-room, your desk, the proximity to this person, where Ms. Walton is. Have a very clear picture of the class-room and the test.
8. Describe Ms. Walton. Use lots of detail.
9. Describe Olivia. Use lots of detail.
10. What is a photographic memory? Do research so you really understand it.
11. Are there any more questions that you can ask yourself?
12. Write an autobiography for this character. Build your character a life.
13. Remember the magic "if." What would you do if you were in this situation?

✎ **WRITE OUT** all of your answers. Be specific. It will get you closer to the truth of the scene, and you will create a stronger character.

⏳ **TIME YOURSELF.** This monologue was written to be about one minute long.

The Funk

Boy or Girl

COMEDIC

It's seriously like that, every single day, the same thing. I wake up, I lay there trying to decide if I should even bother getting out of bed. Then I decide I should get up, but I really would rather stay there in bed. See, I'm already battling with myself and my eyes have only been open for ten seconds. One day I might decide that no, I should just stay right here in this bed. Then, I get up and I stumble around in this … funk for a while. My dad says "funk." That's not a bad word is it? He says it all the time. He says, "The car sounds funky," or he says that something in the fridge smells funky. He's always yelling that. So if it's bad, I'm sorry. So then I get to the bathroom and my sister Ann is in there with the door locked, of course. She knows we have to get in there. There's a curtain on the shower. Just pull the curtain shut. I can still use the toilet or whatever. My brother sometimes brushes his teeth and spits into the kitchen sink. That is just gross. God only knows where he goes pee. And there is never anything to eat either. I mean, I … I'm in a funk. That's all.

CHALLENGE: Speed. This kid talks fast, but it is important to make every word clear. Your thoughts jump around quite fast. Make sure your audience is following you through the whole monologue. Slow down whenever the punctuation asks you to (ellipsis). Dare to take this one on!

1. What is this monologue about?
2. Where are you?
3. Who are you talking to? This question is very important for this monologue.
4. What was your moment before?
5. What do you want? How are you going to get it?
6. Describe your entire house, especially the rooms you mention (bedroom, bathroom, kitchen).
7. How do you get woken up in the morning? Describe the entire process?
8. Describe your family. You didn't mention your mother. Is she around? Are you poor? What does your father do for a living? Use a lot of detail to make us see your family.
9. Describe your "funk." What is at the root of it? Are you unhappy? Frustrated? Angry?
10. Where do you live? City? Country? How is this life different from your own life? What do you have in common with this character's situation? Find differences.
11. Are there any more questions that you can ask yourself?
12. Write an autobiography for this character. Build your character a life.
13. Remember the magic "if." What would *you* do if you were in this situation?

✐ **WRITE OUT** all of your answers. Be specific. It will get you closer to the truth of the scene, and you will create a stronger character.

⧗ **TIME YOURSELF.** This monologue was written to be about one minute long.

COMEDIC

The Sales Pitch

Boy or Girl

So Vera and I got everything set-up. We've done all the work! We called and found out when they open and when they close. 9:00 to 9:00, by the way. And we found out that the concession stand is open too, but they only have snacks and soda. They have Dr. Pepper, Joshua! Entrance fee is $20, ride all day. And we got directions! It will take two hours, 10 minutes to get there. So, here is what we need everyone to do. First, we need to see what kind of car we will take and then we can decide how many people can go. We prefer a van so we can all go. That's you, Chris and George. Ask your mother if she can drive us in your van. Cool? Then, who should go? Vera and I are definitely going since we made all the arrangements and everything. And guys, this is really important. We need to see if there is any way that you guys could pay our way. Normally we do everything for free, like putting this together, but it took a lot of our time to get all this information, get you guys here, and hold this meeting. And both of us spent all that time on the arrangements for the sleepover at Katie's house too. So who's in?

CHALLENGE: You need to be a salesman/woman. Sales pitches are hard because you have to make what you are selling sound so good, even when it isn't. You need to hit people over the head with your idea so that they will buy it no matter what. That takes a strong voice, passion, and a belief in what you are selling. Talk fast, but not too fast.

1. What is this monologue about?
2. Where are you? This is your environment (smell, feel, see, hear). Be very specific. When you look around, what do you see?
3. Who are you talking to? You are talking to a group of boys and girls. Have names and faces for all of them.
4. What was your moment before? What happened just before you began speaking?
5. Who Vera? Describe her in detail.
6. Where is it you want to get everyone to go? A park? Describe it totally.
7. Where were you and Vera when you were making the phone calls and gathering information?
8. We assume Chris and George are brothers? Brother and sister? Describe them.
9. Who is Katie? What kind of "arrangements" did you have to make for that sleepover?
10. Give an example of another time you and Vera have tried to talk your friends into something. Why do they go along with you?
11. Are there any more questions that you can ask yourself?
12. Write an autobiography for this character. Build your character a life.
13. Remember the magic "if." What would *you* do if you were in this situation?

✏ **WRITE OUT** all of your answers. Be specific. It will get you closer to the truth of the scene, and you will create a stronger character.

⧗ **TIME YOURSELF.** This monologue was written to be about one minute long.

The Horseback Rider

Boy or Girl

COMEDIC

What I would suggest is this. Now I'm no expert, but I would say that horseback riding may not be your thing. Isn't this the third time you broke your arm? I know it was your wrist that one time, but I've got news for you. Your wrist is on your arm. Like right on the bottom of your arm. If you don't start being more careful you are going to get a reputation as that kid that is always in a cast. Like Oliver Herndon. Oliver is always hurt. Kid has crutches in every size. I think he has knee problems, though, and has a lot of operations, but the dude is always limping around. If he isn't in a cast or on crutches, he is limping. I cannot think of Oliver Herndon without thinking of his closet filled with crutches. I don't want that for you. Not to mention you're going to have scars all over you. I know scars add character. You said that after you cut your forehead on the barn door. But you have to be a little more careful. After a while too many scars change from character to creepy. Don't go getting all creepy on me. We still have lots of stuff to do together.

CHALLENGE: To be a friend that is sensitive, but who says very insensitive things. You sort of have to be funny to pull this off, otherwise it just sounds like you are making fun of Oliver and putting your friend down. You are a little clueless really. But clueless characters are very fun to play and get a lot of laughs. See the humor in what you are saying and play it straight. Don't go for the laughs, just believe everything you say and your cluelessness will shine through!

1. What is this monologue about?
2. Where are you? This is your environment (smell, feel, see, hear). Be very specific. When you look around, what do you see? Are you visiting your friend in the hospital? At home? Are you in school?
3. Who are you talking to? This is a friend obviously, but it is your responsibility to have a very clear picture of the friend you are talking to. Describe the friend and your relationship.
4. What was your moment before? What happened just before you began speaking? Has your friend just finished telling you what happened? Is your friend just out of surgery?
5. Please describe Oliver Herndon. Have a very clear image of him. When you see Oliver, we want to see Oliver too.
6. How did your friend break her arm? Write out details. Describe how she hurt herself before.
7. Describe the scars already on your friend, especially the one on her forehead.
8. What kind of stuff do you still have to do together?
9. Draw a picture of a closet filled with crutches.
10. Do you, the actor, have any friends that are always hurt? Describe them.
11. Are there any more questions that you can ask yourself?
12. Write an autobiography for this character. Build your character a life.
13. Remember the magic "if." What would you do if you were in this situation?

✎ **WRITE OUT** all of your answers. Be specific. It will get you closer to the truth of the scene, and you will create a stronger character.

⏲ **TIME YOURSELF.** This monologue was written to be about one minute long.

COMEDIC

Baby   Girl

We had to carry around a bag of flour for a whole week pretending it was a baby. I was like, one week? Shoot. But…guys in school were all like, "Nice baby! Who's the daddy? It looks like Dante." Which was so stupid because it didn't look anything like Dante. And, besides that, I've never even kissed Dante. Then I see Dante and he says, "Ain't there something we need to talk about?" I told him, "Get lost unless you want me to break this flour-baby over top of your head!" Then he goes, he goes, "If you hit me and I get that flour all over me, I will look like that baby's daddy!" I just said, "Shut up!" (Pause) I don't know if you did the flour-baby thing when you were in school. I never heard you say anything if you did. But it's hard. I just think a real baby would be easier than the flour-baby because everyone will just like leave you alone and everyone won't be saying stuff. Just be a lot more peaceful if it was a real baby. And a real baby would let you know when it wants something. With the flour-baby we just had to pretend it was hungry. If they cry or fuss, you either feed them or change them. Now that . . .that seems easy.

CHALLENGE: You have a lot of quotation marks within this monologue. When you have quotation marks, you have to change your voice to sound like who's talking. You have to be a group of boys at one point, and you have to be Dante at another point. That can be tricky. Plus, this teenager obviously missed the point of the lesson. You have to be bright to pull off 'not- so-bright.' Make all the people in the monologue real to you.

1. What is this monologue about?
2. Where are you? This is your environment (smell, feel, see, hear). Be very specific.
3. Who are you talking to? An older sister? A friend no longer in school because she got pregnant? Be creative with this one.
4. What was your moment before? What happened just before you began speaking?
5 What do you want? How are you going to get it?
6. Who is Dante? Describe him. Why does everyone say that it looks like Dante? Do you guys have a crush on each other? Do you flirt? Try it with a secret crush and see if it changes anything in the monologue?
7. Describe everything you had to do with the bag of flour. How does this lesson work? If you've never heard of it, look it up. Do you think this is a good lesson for girls? Boys?
8. Have you ever spent time with a real baby? Describe it in detail. Did you enjoy it? Where were you?
9. Describe the boys who were picking on you about the baby? Were they your friends? Just boys from school?
10. Describe the teacher that gave you this assignment.
11. Are there any more questions that you can ask yourself?
12. Write an autobiography for this character. Build your character a life.
13. Remember the magic "if." What would you do if you were in this situation?

✎ **WRITE OUT** all of your answers. Be specific. It will get you closer to the truth of the scene, and you will create a stronger character.

⏳ **TIME YOURSELF.** This monologue was written to be about one minute long.

Kim Kardashian Girl

I saw it! This lady looks just like her, just like Kim Kardashian! The same face, the same body, the same hair. Everything! Then I heard someone say that the other lady might have had surgery to *look* like Kim Kardashian. Just imagine that! Here you are, someone who looks like you. I mean, you look the way you were born to look. And someone has surgery to look just like you. How could you, I mean, what would that person tell the doctor? Make me look just like Kim Kardashian? What? What if, what if you wanted to look like someone who wasn't famous? Say if *you* wanted to look like *me*. I know you don't, but what would you do? Bring in a picture of me? But how could you... what could be *wrong* with you to want that? To look like someone else? You would have to totally hate yourself, right? What if everybody just got surgery to look like someone else? Would we, would we...wait! (Pause) Would we finally all look like the same person? We would all eventually look the same! Think about that!

CHALLENGE: Speed and annunciation. This should be a one minute monologue. Read it and practice it until you can do it in one minute. If that is entirely too fast for you, choose another monologue. You need to recognize your punctuation and use it properly. Exclaim! Pause. Change the thought on the ellipsis. A period is like a pause, when you are highly excited. You must change your voice levels or the monologue will be fast and boring. Go for it!

1. What is this monologue about?
2. Where are you? This is your environment (smell, feel, see, hear). Be very specific. When you look around, what do you see?
3. Who are you talking to?
4. What was your moment before? What happened just before you began speaking?
5. Where did you "see" this story? Have a clear picture of where you saw it, where you were when you saw it, and who was around.
6. You said you heard someone say that the other woman may have had surgery to look like Kim Kardashian. Who said that? Where were you? Do you think it's true?
7. Think about plastic surgery. Describe how you think a doctor does plastic surgery?
8. If a woman would have surgery to look like Kim Kardashian, who would a man have surgery to look like? Why do you say that?
9. If you could change anything about yourself, what would you change? Why? If you could look like anyone in the world, whom would you want to look like? How is that person different from you?
10. Try doing this monologue very slowly, like really slow. Did you discover anything doing that? How did it change the character?
11. Are there any more questions that you can ask yourself?
12. Write an autobiography for this character. Build your character a life.
13. Remember the magic "if." What would *you* do if you were in this situation?

✎ **WRITE OUT** all of your answers. Be specific. It will get you closer to the truth of the scene, and you will create a stronger character.

⏳ **TIME YOURSELF.** This monologue was written to be about one minute long.

COMEDIC

Venting

Girl

(Hopping on one foot) OMG! I stubbed my toe *so* bad! I think I broke it. I know I did. Dang it! That hurt so much. Why did God make toes? OW! (Off a look) Quit laughing! Why is that stupid table there in the first place? Get your ugly feet off of it! I hate brothers! I hate this stupid house! (Long pause. Calming down) Do you realize you play that stupid game all day long? Seriously. Your brain is going to turn into grits! Grits for brains! You and all your friends. All you do is stare at that screen and occasionally laugh at me when I hurt myself. You're like a robot. You and Ricardo and Stephen. When was the last time you guys did anything in the way of exercise? I am a cheerleader. I dance. I swim. You? Nothing. You sit on your butt and play your game. It's gross. (Pause) I'm going to my room. Enjoy your game. I hope you and your robot friends stub all your toes off. (As you limp off) If I can find matches, I am torching that table.

CHALLENGE: You're hurt. But it's also an injury that we all experience and it isn't that critical. It's the end of the world when you've done it, but it doesn't last long and we all know it. So it makes it kind of funny when someone else does it. You need to really over react at first, then come all the way back. Then you start picking on your brother probably because he laughed at you. You are unloading on him and it is really for no reason. Then leave, talking as you go. Trust your punctuation and it should be very funny.

1. What is this monologue about?
2. Where are you? Describe the area clearly so you can see it. This is your environment. Make it clear for us.
3. Who are you talking to? It's your brother, but who is he? What is your relationship with him?
4. What was your moment before? What happened just before you said these words? You stubbed your toe. Where were you headed? How did it happen?
5. What do you want? How are you going to get it?
6. Who is Ricardo and Stephen? Have a clear picture of who they are in your mind.
7. What game does your brother play? Describe it.
8. Where is everyone else in your family? What time of day is it?
9. What are you going to do when you go to your room? Have something in mind, even if it's falling on your bed and Snapchatting friends.
10. What kind of dance classes do you take? What kind of swimming do you do?
11. Are there any more questions that you can ask yourself?
12. Write an autobiography for this character. Build your character a life.
13. Remember the magic "if." What would *you* do if you were in this situation?

🖉 **WRITE OUT** all of your answers. Be specific. It will get you closer to the truth of the scene, and you will create a stronger character.

⏳ **TIME YOURSELF.** This monologue was written to be about one minute long.

Excuses

Girl

COMEDIC

I know you asked us to have the assignment done today. But I got a little problem with that. I mean, it started as a little problem, but then it turned into a huge problem. Please do not say that my excuses are no longer accepted. You haven't even heard this one yet. I mean, this isn't an excuse. Well, it is an excuse but…wait? Is it still considered an excuse even if it's the truth? Please don't look at me like that. (Pause) You know my dog Rex, right? No he didn't eat it this time! Okay, so, Rex and me go outside and there is a squirrel, right? And Rex pulls really hard. He's big, Rex is, and he dragged me and I fell into the disgusting ditch! Well, I can't swim and there was a lot of water in the ditch, right? I mean, not that much, but it only takes like a teaspoon of water. You told us that, right? And I imagine you meant a teaspoon of fresh water, not ditch water, right? So, here's the thing. Well, my homework was in my pocket so I wouldn't forget to bring it today. (Holds up a dirty, ripped piece of paper.) You probably want me to do it over and turn it in tomorrow, right?

CHALLENGE: To speak fast, but slow enough so your audience can follow along. You are trying to make it sound really awful so your teacher will buy it. But, you are also lying. Make it sensational, but keep it honest. Lying is an art. If you are not a liar, which I hope you are not, this is a great test for you. Give it a try!

1. What is this monologue about?
2. Where are you? This is your environment (smell, feel, see, hear). Be very specific.
3. Who are you talking to? Describe the teacher completely.
4. What was your moment before? What happened just before you began speaking?
5. What do you want? How are you going to get it?
6. Describe Rex. Describe his leash, his collar. How big is he? What kind of dog is he?
7. Describe your driveway and the ditch. People in the city don't know what a ditch is. Explain it.
8. What are some other excuses you have tried with your teacher. How does your teacher react to you when you have an excuse? You say, "Don't look at me like that." How is your teacher looking at you?
9. What was the assignment you were supposed to have done? Why didn't you do it?
10. Are there any more questions that you can ask yourself?
11. Write an autobiography for this character. Build your character a life.
12. Remember the magic "if ": What would *you* do if you were in this situation?

✐ **WRITE OUT** all of your answers. Be specific. It will get you closer to the truth of the scene, and you will create a stronger character.

⧗ **TIME YOURSELF.** This monologue was written to be about one minute long.

COMEDIC

The Dress   Girl

You don't know anything about fashion, dad! NOTHING! This dress was not even that expensive. It's not like it's a Prada. It's Rebecca Taylor for crying out loud. What did you expect? That I would come home with crap? Mossimo? Eclair? You want me to hit up Target for my clothes, dad? You dropped me at Nordstrom's. What did you expect me to do, walk down to Target? The Leskos can get their clothes at Target. You want me to look like Lindsay Lesko, dad? The girl you were making fun of at the movie. Or her sister, the one that looks like she shops at Goodwill? You'd freak if I dressed like that. I would never … I don't understand you. You gave me your card and dropped me at Nordstrom's. You knew I was going to shop! The last time it was all fine when I was with your girlfriend. What was it… Brittany? Brianna! As long as it was impressing Brianna it was fine, right? But now you're all bent out of shape because of a dress? It's a dress! Why wouldn't I buy it? I should look good. And this dress is hot, so I bought it. So just stop it or I'm leaving!

CHALLENGE: To be a convincing spoiled brat. Some people will hear this and not think it's funny. What is funny is that this character is so spoiled she doesn't even realize how she sounds. It is also challenging to speak in a heightened state. You need to be sure it isn't all on the same note and pace. It will be too grating to listen to you if you do that. Pause here and there.

1. What is this monologue about?
2. Where are you? This is your environment (smell, feel, see, hear). Be very specific. When you look around, what do you see? Are you still in the car? Are you home?
3. Who are you talking to? You are obviously talking to your father, but what is he like? He must be single because you mention a girlfriend. What kind of man is he?
4. What was your moment before? What happened just before you began speaking? Did he see the receipt? Did you tell him how much the dress cost? Did the purchase appear on his phone?
5. Describe the dress. Use details. Why did you need a dress like this?
6. Who are the Leskos? How do you know them?
7. Describe the night your father saw the Leskos at the movies. Where did he see Lindsay? What did he say about her?
8. Who is Brianna? Describe her. Did you like her being with your father? What kind of relationship did you have with her? What did you buy the day you shopped with her?
9. Describe the walk you would have to do to get from Nordstrom to Target. Make it up in your mind. If you can see the walk, your audience will see the walk.
10. If you are unfamiliar with the brand names you are talking about, do research. Look up Mossimo, Eclair, Prada and Rebecca Taylor. Know what you are talking about.
11. Are there any more questions that you can ask yourself?
12. Write an autobiography for this character. Build your character a life.
13. Remember the magic "if." What would *you* do if you were in this situation?

✐ **WRITE OUT** all of your answers. Be specific. It will get you closer to the truth of the scene, and you will create a stronger character.

⧗ **TIME YOURSELF.** This monologue was written to be about one minute long.

The Only Boy

Boy

COMEDIC

Are you listening? I am the only boy in my acting class! I'm the only boy in my dance class too! What is wrong with you guys? Do you seriously have no interest in being where the girls are? Sasha's in there. Corrine is in there. Toni, Rhonda. The new girl Allie is in my dance class. She is so cute. And she is a great dancer. These girls are partnered up with girls because I'm the only guy. And honestly, I'm a horrible dancer! The girls being guys are so much better than I am. The class needs guys. The cutest girls in our class are in acting and dance classes. Am I missing something? Are you guys so out of touch that you long to be single? (Long pause) Oh man. Fine. Okay. I will just go on being the only one. And when Corrine says to me, like she did yesterday, "How come Devan and Lane don't want to be actors? Actors are so awesome." I'll just have to say, "Well Corrine, I guess they would just rather go home and play video games and Snapchat stupid faces at each other." (Pause) Really? Okay. Don't expect me to introduce you to Allie either. Just because she is the cutest girl in school.

CHALLENGE: You are talking to a few people (at least two). You need to look like you are talking to multiple people. Without practice, this can really throw you. Place the people very specifically in front of you and make eye contact with each imaginary person. You are also using a lot of names. Be careful and go slow enough so your audience can stay with you.

1. What is this monologue about?
2. Where are you? This is your environment (smell, feel, see, hear). Be very specific. When you look around, what do you see? How can a different environment add to this scene?
3. Who are you talking to? You are talking to at least two people (Devan and Lane). Who are they? Be specific. Put a name and a face to each one of them.
4. What was your moment before? What happened just before you began speaking? How did this scene get set?
5. Why do you want your friends to join the class? You are using the presence of the girls to try and convince your friends to join. Why? Think carefully about it.
6. Please tell us all about Sasha, Corrine, Toni, Rhonda and Allie. Describe them until you can picture them completely, so they are clear in your mind when you speak of them.
7. Tell us about your acting class. Do these girls like you in there? Are you friends with them outside of class?
8. Describe your dance class. You said you are a horrible dancer. Are you, the actor, a bad dancer? Do you like to dance? Is it easy for you to picture yourself in a dance class?
9. These are your friends and you know your friends play video games and use Snapchat. That probably means you do, too. What video games do you play? Who do you Snapchat with?
10. Are there any more questions that you can ask yourself?
11. Write an autobiography for this character. Build your character a life.
12. Remember the magic "if." What would *you* do if you were in this situation?

✏ **WRITE OUT** all of your answers. Be specific. It will get you closer to the truth of the scene, and you will create a stronger character.

⏳ **TIME YOURSELF.** This monologue was written to be about one minute long.

COMEDIC

Advice

Boy

I'M OVER IT! That's how you do it. You tell her, "Sweetheart"… do you call her sweetheart? No wait. You call her Coconut. Why on earth do you call her– never mind. It doesn't matter. It's sickening, but it doesn't matter. Just listen. You say, "Coconut, I'm over it. I think you are really swell." (Off his reaction) Swell. What's wrong with swell? It's like, kind of a combination of sweet and well. Okay fine. Say *great*. "Coconut, I'm over it. I think you are really great, but this bus stops here. Get out." (Off his look) I know it seems harsh. I knew you were going to say that. But listen, if you don't let her down hard, she'll just keep coming around. She'll put notes in your locker, she'll give you half of her bologna sandwich. It will never end. Tell her this. Tell her you have a friend that thinks she's really special (Off his look) I … I'm not too proud to step into your shoes, bro. What can I say? I think she's swell.

CHALLENGE: Three times you have to change mid-sentence, based on a look you are getting from the person you are talking to. That can be tricky. You need to pause, observe, then go on. Plus, you are being sneaky. Don't let your audience know your true intention is to get the girl for yourself. This should be fun.

1. What is this monologue about?
2. Where are you? Be specific. Try it in a couple of different places – on the bus, in the locker room, in the library.
3. Who are you talking to? Obviously it is a friend you know well who has a girlfriend you are interested in. Thoroughly describe the person. Clearly describe your relationship.
4. What was your moment before? What happened just before you said these words?
5. What do you want? How are you going to get it?
6. Who is this girl you are talking about? Be very specific. What do you like about her?
7. Are you experienced with letting girls down or are you just trying to get your friend to break up with her so you can date her? Be clear. Are you manipulating or telling the truth?
8. When your direction is, "off his look," what is his look? Practice different looks in the mirror so you can have a clear image of his looks.
9. Describe your school. Is it a large school? Small? Private? Tell us about it.
10. Describe the perfect girl for you. Is she just like this girl? What is the difference?
11. Are there any more questions that you can ask yourself?
12. Write an autobiography for this character. Build your character a life.
13. Remember the magic "if." What would *you* do if you were in this situation?

✐ **WRITE OUT** all of your answers. Be specific. It will get you closer to the truth of the scene, and you will create a stronger character.

⧖ **TIME YOURSELF.** This monologue was written to be about one minute long.

A Man of Leisure

Boy

COMEDIC

I was walking back from the pool at my complex and my mom came out of the laundry room and she said, "Well aren't you just a man of leisure." I asked her what that was supposed to mean and she told me to get a job. I reminded her that I was only 14-years-old. "Your cousin is delivering papers. You could borrow a bike and deliver papers." That's what she said. Borrow a bike and deliver papers! Crazy right? Little did she know that I had already gone down to The Star in June. I figured I'd look. It would get me out of the apartment at least. So they told me that I could do it, but part of the job is collecting overdue bills from customers. I said okay. He said, "Great! Your first stop is your mother's apartment." I said, "What?" He says, "Yeah, your mother hasn't paid her bill in five months. You can start with her." I told him that would be tough because I don't think my mom has any money. He says, "Fine. We'll take her paper bill out of your first paycheck." I told him I didn't have a bike and I left. Man of leisure. Yeah, right.

CHALLENGE: You are imitating people. You imitate your mother and the guy at The Star. That means you have to change your voice and your speed. And when it is more than one person, it can be tricky. It should be really funny if you can pull it off. Give it a go!

1. What is this monologue about?
2. Where are you? This is your environment (smell, feel, see, hear). Be very specific. When you look around, what do you see? How can you make your environment add to this scene?
3. Who are you talking to? You are talking about something that happened with your mother, but who are you talking to?
4. What was your moment before? What happened just before you began speaking? How did this scene get set?
5. Describe your mother. Does she have a job? What is she like? You don't mention your father. Is he around? Are they divorced?
6. It is safe to assume you live in an apartment complex. Describe your apartment and the complex. Where is the laundry room that your mother was in? Draw the complex to give yourself a clear picture.
7. Who is the guy at The Star? Completely describe him. Fat? Skinny? Rude? Nice? What was he like?
8. You never told your mother about going to The Star to get a job. Why didn't you tell her?
9. What were you wearing when your mother came out of the laundry room and called you a man of leisure?
10. Are there any more questions that you can ask yourself?
11. Write an autobiography for this character. Build your character a life
12. Remember the magic "if." What would *you* do if you were in this situation?

✎ **WRITE OUT** all of your answers. Be specific. It will get you closer to the truth of the scene, and you will create a stronger character.

⧗ **TIME YOURSELF.** This monologue was written to be about one minute long.

COMEDIC

Dancing

Boy

I know you guys have been wondering what I have been up to. I need you to promise you won't laugh (Pause) Seriously? You won't promise? (Pause) Fine. I need you to at least promise you won't tell Isabelle? You cannot tell Isabelle! (Pause) I've been taking dance lessons. (Pause) Get it all out guys, but when we get to the Gentlemen's Invitational Dance, I will be able to do this (He dances, as though he as a girl in his arms. He is bad at it.) One-two-three, one-two-three, one-two-three, one-two-three. And this: (Dances again. Badly.) One-two-three-four, one-two-three-four, one-two-three-four, one-two-three-four. And even this: (Dances freestyle very badly) Lada-dee, lada-dum, como-se, como-sum, bada-bing, bada-bum, dee-dee-dee, dee-dee-dum- (He stops. His friends are laughing). I really don't care, guys. Laugh your butts off. You'll see who gets attention at the dance. You'll see.

CHALLENGE: You have to dance. Badly. It should be very funny if you can pull it off. You are also talking to multiple people. That can be difficult. Figure out where they are standing (preferably toward your audience) and be specific. Really milk the dance numbers. Dare to be silly, but don't overdo it. Just be bad. And if you can be out of rhythm, even better. GO FOR IT!

1. What is this monologue about?
2. Where are you? This is your environment. Are you in the hallway at school? Cafeteria? Somewhere outside of school? Be specific.
3. Who are you talking to? Describe the guys you are talking to with great detail.
4. What was your moment before? What happened just before you said these words?
5. What do you want? How are you going to get it?
6. Who is Isabelle? Be specific. Describe her in detail.
7. Where do you take dance lessons? With whom? Be specific.
8. Describe a dance lesson. How do lessons go?
9. What is the Gentlemen's Invitational Dance? Where is it held? Tell us all about it. Have you ever been before?
10. What have you been missing while you were talking dance lessons? What have your friends been up to without you?
11. Are there any more questions that you can ask yourself?
12. Write an autobiography for this character. Build your character a life.
13. Remember the magic "if." What would you do if you were in this situation?

✐ **WRITE OUT** all of your answers. Be specific. It will get you closer to the truth of the scene, and you will create a stronger character.

⧗ **TIME YOURSELF.** This monologue was written to be about one minute long.

Here We Go Again

Boy

Here we go again! Every single time there's girls around, this story comes up and it's always you that brings it up, Kev. I'll just say it. I peed my pants during a little league game! There, Kev, I beat you to it. (To the girls) And right on cue, you're laughing. Sure, why not? No Kevin, I got this. Then Kevin would come in right here with, "And he started crying and ran off the field!" And, (To the girls) you all laugh even harder. Of course! It's hilarious! Go ahead, laughs on me! (Pause) Then, when you slowly stop laughing, (Pause) when you guys finally realize it isn't that funny and you quit laughing, (Long pause) Oh, come on. Kevin, you suck. I hate you. (Starts to leave, then turns back.) No. I'm staying. Because every time I leave, I hear everyone laugh even harder, so I'm just staying this time. (Pause) I'm not leaving, so go right ahead and laugh your heads off. (Pause. Turns and runs off.) I HATE ALL OF YOU!

CHALLENGE: The pauses. You must make your audience see the girls and actually hear them laughing. If YOU really see them and hear them, then we will to. This monologue should be fun to do. You are making fun of yourself. Have a great time with it!

1. What is this monologue about?
2. Where are you?
3. Who are you talking to? Have images for all the girls. This question is very important for this monologue.
4. What was your moment before?
5. What do you want? How are you going to get it?
6. Why did you pee your pants in that game? Was that something that happened to this character often?
7. Did you play Little League? Picture the field. What position were you playing? Were you batting? Where did you run to?
8. How did everyone react at the game when you ran off?
9. Who is Kevin? Was he at the game? Was he a teammate? Why do you hang out with someone who is going to embarrass you?
10. What do you think happened after this moment? Did you come back? Does the embarrassment wear off?
11. Are there any more questions that you can ask yourself?
12. Write an autobiography for this character. Build your character a life.
13. Remember the magic "if." What would *you* do if you were in this situation?

✏ **WRITE OUT** all of your answers. Be specific. It will get you closer to the truth of the scene, and you will create a stronger character.

⧖ **TIME YOURSELF.** This monologue was written to be about one minute long.

Notes & Thoughts

DRAMATIC
Monologues

DRAMATIC

Empathy   Boy or Girl

Why are you guys always mentioning that she was adopted? Why are you so obsessed with that? Cut her some slack. She sneaks a beer at the party and you guys are all, like, her parents were drunks! She's a drunk! Zach, I saw you drink a beer at that party, too. We didn't all go, "Zach's an alcoholic!" Just chill! If she knew that you guys were secretly judging her, she would be so hurt. Just stop doing it. (Pause) And stop trying to talk her into finding her real parents, Kayla. Just because you would "need to look them in the eyes," doesn't mean Willow does. She's happy. She has a wonderful home. She is loved like crazy. You've been there. They love her so much. And she has great friends. At least she thinks she does. It could be a really painful experience to meet your biological parents. What if they are really bad people? Or worse, what if they are dead? Just try those shoes on for a minute and see if you would like to go on a search for the total strangers who put you up for adoption. Just think about that.

CHALLENGE: To not preach. Why? Because preaching can tend to be on just one note and that is annoying to listen to. You are trying to teach your friends a lesson, but it has to be very heartfelt. Allow for pauses. Allow your audience time to hear your message. There is a good message in here.

1. What is this monologue about?
2. Where are you? This is your environment (smell, feel, see, hear). Be very specific.
3. Who are you talking to? Be specific. Three friends? Four? Describe Zach and Kayla.
4. What was your moment before? What happened just before you began speaking?
5. What do you want? How are you going to get it?
6. Describe Willow. Be very specific. She is the main subject of this monologue. Make sure we see her by creating a very strong image of her: Her home, her parents. Let us see it.
7. Tell us about another time when these friends judged Willow. Do they judge everyone? Why are you fed-up?
8. Tell us about the party where there was alcohol. Share the image of her sneaking a beer and Zach drinking.
9. Do you, the actor, have any friends that were adopted? Share. Would you want to find your biological parents if you were adopted? Why or why not?
10. How do you know that Willow's adoptive parents love her so much? Give examples.
11. Are there any more questions that you can ask yourself?
12. Write an autobiography for this character. Build your character a life.
13. Remember the magic "if." What would *you* do if you were in this situation?

✎ **WRITE OUT** all of your answers. Be specific. It will get you closer to the truth of the scene, and you will create a stronger character.

⧖ **TIME YOURSELF.** This monologue was written to be about one minute long.

DRAMATIC

Meat   Boy or Girl

I DON'T WANT IT! Why do you insist? I can't do it! Plain and simple! It's an animal. I don't eat animals. I can't say it any other way to make you understand me better. I don't eat animals! There is plenty of food to eat that is not an animal. I'll eat these beans. I like beans. I like potatoes. I just don't … And don't you dare accuse me of trying to make a statement. If I was going to make a statement, I would be telling you about how cruel it is to farm animals for our own satisfaction. That animals have souls and animals love and they care and they feel pain. I could tell you that we don't *need* the protein from meat. That's your big argument. You can get protein from mushrooms or Brussels sprouts or broccoli or peas or spinach. OR KALE! EAT KALE! *That* would be making a statement! Criticizing *you* for eating meat would be making a statement! But I don't do that. Go right ahead and eat it. I am completely satisfied with everything else that is on this table. In fact, it looks delicious. Thank you for preparing it.

CHALLENGE: Annunciation. You are saying a mouthful and it is emotionally charged. You need to speak clearly and annunciate properly. This topic is obviously one you care deeply about and think about often. Your love of animals is at the base of everything you have to say. These words should sound like they just fall out of your mouth every time you open it. Work hard. Know what you are talking about and let it fly!

1. What is this monologue about?
2. Where are you? This is your environment (smell, feel, see, hear). Be very specific. When you look around, what do you see? It seems you are at a table. Where is it? Be clear.
3. Who are you talking to? It seems logical that it would be whomever normally prepares your food. Mother? Father? What if it were a grandparent? Or what if you were away at camp? Or lived in a group home? Try it with different people.
4. What was your moment before? What happened just before you began speaking? Be specific. Something set you off.
5. What do you want? How are you going to get it?
6. How do you, the actor, feel about eating meat? Is this monologue one you can relate to?
7. Describe another time you had to defend your stance on not eating meat.
8. Do some research. Is farming animals really cruel? Can you get proper protein from vegetables? Know what you are talking about. It will help you believe it.
9. Why do you think the person serving you is insistent about you eating meat? Why is this an argument again and again? Elaborate.
10. So, does this character eat fish? What do you think of the argument that many people will eat fish but not meat?
11. Are there any more questions that you can ask yourself?
12. Write an autobiography for this character. Build your character a life.
13. Remember the magic "if." What would *you* do if you were in this situation?

✐ **WRITE OUT** all of your answers. Be specific. It will get you closer to the truth of the scene, and you will create a stronger character.

⏳ **TIME YOURSELF.** This monologue was written to be about one minute long.

41

DRAMATIC

What is Happening? Boy or Girl

I… I can't breath. When it happens, I can't breath. It feels like someone is holding me down, pressing on my chest. I can't catch my breath. (Pause) This happened yesterday, too. Maybe the day before that, too. If I'm around people, not you, but if I'm around a bunch of people, I just start to feel like the walls are coming in closer, like the room is shrinking. And the voices of all the people, they like begin to. . . to wind or grind or screech. It's unpleasant and it. . . it hurts my head. And I look at everyone and no one notices the walls closing-in on us and no one notices the screeching sound of the voices and I just want to scream but. . . but I can't because I know people will look at me and think … Then I saw Olin and he was laughing so hard, but it sounded so scary like. . . like (scary laughter) and I just started crying. And I couldn't stop crying. So I ran away. I just ran away and waited for it to stop. Then I called you.

CHALLENGE: Speed and control. When you do a monologue and the character seems to be a bit unstable, your natural tendency is to go too fast. Resist going too fast. Stay in control. You are not in the troubled state of mind right now, but the memory of it is fresh and it is frightening. Remembering it in front of us will be terrifying enough. This is a tough piece, so GO FOR IT!

1. What is this monologue about?
2. Where are you? This is your environment (smell, feel, see, hear). Be very specific. When you look around, what do you see?
3. Who are you talking to? Who did you call? A parent? A friend? A teacher?
4. What was your moment before? What happened just before you began speaking? Remember, you had to wait for this person to get to you, so what did you do while you waited?
5. Describe exactly where you were when you began to feel the walls closing in. Be specific.
6. You say you look at everyone. Who are you looking at? Who was there?
7. Who is Olin?
8. What do those screeching, winding voices sound like? Have a horrible sound in your head when you talk about them.
9. You mention that it happened yesterday, too. What happened yesterday to cause it to happen? Where were you? And the day before that?
10. What are you afraid people will think?
11. Are there any more questions that you can ask yourself?
12. Write an autobiography for this character. Build your character a life.
13. Remember the magic "if." What would *you* do if you were in this situation?

🖋 **WRITE OUT** all of your answers. Be specific. It will get you closer to the truth of the scene, and you will create a stronger character.

⏳ **TIME YOURSELF.** This monologue was written to be about one minute long.

DRAMATIC

My Brother   Boy or Girl

Um… I'm not sure I understand the question. I mean, I heard your question. I guess I'm just not sure why you would, why you would be asking me that. (Pause) Of course I loved my brother. He was my brother. (Pause) That's just a technique, right? You are just trying to … You want me to talk to you about how I feel, right? (Pause) I, I'm afraid to. . . to talk about that. My father always ignored James so we almost never talk about James at home. So James never wanted to come home because my father would … he was so dumb, my father. Sometimes James would be right in the middle of saying something. He would be so happy and he would just be talking and laughing so hard. And he wasn't talking about being gay or anything either. He would just be talking and me and my mom would be laughing and my dad, he would just get up and leave the room. Right in the middle. And my brother would, it would just … My brother must have died a thousand times before he died.

CHALLENGE: Pauses. You have three in this monologue. Pauses have to be filled with thoughts and images. If you cannot do that with this piece, don't do this piece. This is highly emotional, but the actor, the best he or she can, is keeping the emotions bottled-up. If and when the emotion can no longer be contained and bubbles out, that is when you have it. Very difficult monologue.

1. What is this monologue about?
2. Where are you? This is your environment (smell, feel, see, hear). Be very specific.
3. Who are you talking to?
4. What was your moment before? What happened just before you began speaking?
5. What do you want? How are you going to get it?
6. Describe your brother. Use as many details as you can think of. Is he your only sibling?
7. What happened to your brother? Don't shy away from current times and events.
8. Describe your father. Whether or not you are using your own father's image, describe this   man in detail.
9. Describe your mother. Did she understand your brother? Tell a story about that to prove it.
10. Describe a room in which you saw your father get up and walk away from your brother. Where was everyone sitting? What was the story about? Where did your father go when he left?
11. Are there any more questions that you can ask yourself?
12. Write an autobiography for this character. Build your character a life.
13. Remember the magic "if." What would *you* do if you were in this situation?

✎ **WRITE OUT** all of your answers. Be specific. It will get you closer to the truth of the scene, and you will create a stronger character.

⧗ **TIME YOURSELF.** This monologue was written to be about one minute long.

DRAMATIC

The Fat Lady

Boy or Girl

I told her that's a load of crap! Crap isn't swearing, is it? I didn't say the 'S' word! People say crap all the time. "I have so much crap to do." "Look at all this crap!" So okay, what happened was this lady was right behind us in the line, and she is just rude. The guy in front of us, I think there was something wrong with him. He was buying a big bottle of beer and he's got a bunch of change and he's counting it. This lady behind us is getting so antsy. This guy ends up dropping his money and there are coins going every which way. This poor guy is mumbling and grumbling, his pockets are turned inside out, his hair is all over the place, he's. . . he's not doing so good. A dime rolls over by this fat lady with a cart full of ice cream and she picks it up. The guy holds out his hand and she says, "finder's keepers," and she refuses to give him his dime. So I gave the guy a dime and he paid. He had like two pennies to spare. Then I hear the fat lady tell the woman behind her that it was her dime in the first place. I turned and told her that was a load of crap. That's all I said. I don't know why they called you.

CHALLENGE: Defending yourself without sounding like a jerk. You stood up for one adult and stood up *to* another adult. That is brave and commendable. However, you got in trouble for it. So now you have to make your parents or whoever you are talking to understand your story. You need to spell it out clearly so they understand that this disabled person needed you and the lady in line was wrong and dishonest.

1. What is this monologue about?
2. Where are you?
3. Who are you talking to? Your parents? Your guardian? Who would "they" call?
4. What was your moment before? What happened just before you said these words?
5. What do you want? How are you going to get it?
6. Describe the woman you are talking about. Be very specific in your description so you can picture her fully.
7. Describe the man. See him clearly. Was he homeless? What do you think is wrong with him?
8. Who were you with? You said "us." Were you with a friend? Co-worker? Perhaps you were with someone you were trying to impress?
9. Describe the store you were in. Describe the cashier and the entire surroundings. See it clearly.
10. Who called? Something must have happened between the time you said, "That's a load of crap!" and someone calling. What happened? Is that really what you said?
11. Are there any more questions that you can ask yourself?
12. Write an autobiography for this character. Build your character a life.
13. Remember the magic "if." What would *you* do if you were in this situation?

✐ **WRITE OUT** all of your answers. Be specific. It will get you closer to the truth of the scene, and you will create a stronger character.

⌛ **TIME YOURSELF.** This monologue was written to be about one minute long.

DRAMATIC

Cancer   Boy or Girl

I'm sorry I haven't called you back. It's just... It's been a rough few weeks. I loved hearing about your trip to Europe. It looked awesome. That picture of London was so cool. And you were in Spain too, right? (Off the look) It was, it seemed beautiful. You are really lucky. Your parents take you on the best trips. (Pause) So, um... I... I really don't know how to tell you this. Not just you, I mean I don't know how to tell anybody. I *haven't* told anybody. I just, it's just hard. It's weird. But, so I went to the doctor. Remember I told you I wasn't feeling well? It was just before you went to Europe? Well, I went to the doctor because I wasn't getting any better. And the doctor, Doctor Richardson, is your neighbor actually. It's Dennis Richardson's dad. Well he's my doctor. And he said that I, um, I have Hodgkin's Disease. Do you know what it is? (Pause) Well, it's. . . it's cancer. I have cancer. (Pause) That's the first time I ever said it. But yeah, I have it.

CHALLENGE: To stay with the punctuation. This is a very emotional piece, but you are holding your emotions in. That can be very tricky. You have to believe the punctuation. Fill all the ellipsises with thoughts, and try to be optimistic as you tell someone really bad news about yourself. This is the first time you are telling anyone. It is very hard to say, but you surely will have a sense of relief when you are done. Difficult piece. Try it!

1. What is this monologue about?
2. Where are you? This is your environment (smell, feel, see, hear). Be very specific. When you look around, what do you see?
3. Who are you talking to? This is very important. You must be close, but not too close. Otherwise the person would have known already. But you did tell the person about your illness. How do you know this person?
4. What was your moment before? What happened just before you began speaking? Why are you opening up about this?
5. What do you want? How are you going to get it?
6. How did the doctor tell you about the Hodgkins Disease? Paint a very clear moment for yourself as you think about this. It will help you.
7. Describe your doctor. Make him very clear. And describe his son Dennis.
8. Do research on Hodgkin's Disease. Know as much as you can about it so it can come out through your images.
9. Why is it hard to tell people about the cancer?
10. What was the picture of London? Find one. What was beautiful about it?
11. What have you been doing the last few weeks that has been rough? Have you been crying? Hiding out? Seeing doctors?
12. Are there any more questions that you can ask yourself?
13. Write an autobiography for this character. Build your character a life.
14. Remember the magic "if." What would *you* do if you were in this situation?

✎ **WRITE OUT** all of your answers. Be specific. It will get you closer to the truth of the scene, and you will create a stronger character.

⏱ **TIME YOURSELF.** This monologue was written to be about one minute long.

DRAMATIC

My Vote
Boy or Girl

I want to vote. I know I can't, but I want to. Every commercial on TV is about the election and we don't even have a say in who wins. That sucks. And I can hear the difference between them. I have made a decision on who I would like to vote for. And what's so interesting is that it is such a personal decision, who you vote for. But it's a selfless thing to do, to vote. You are expressing your own personal vote, but you think beyond yourself when you do it. What do you care about? Right? And you vote for the person who most closely represents your views and opinions. Right? I think I'm right. So, I care about the environment. A lot. Our oceans and our rivers and our… land. If it gets warmer, we are all in trouble. I read that myself. Why is that even something we are voting on? And I don't want to get shot. Who does? Why are we voting on taking control of our guns? Why would a gun be allowed in a city by anybody but a policeman? Doesn't that scare everyone? The idea of being shot? It scares me. A lot of things do.

CHALLENGE: To be passionate about something you have no control over. It is tough not to go up into your higher register (head voice) when you get exasperated. You have to fight that urge because it sounds like whining, and nobody likes to hear whining. If you use this piece as an audition piece, you must not get so excited about what you perceive to be something so obvious that you force your point of view on the audience. Be bewildered, but be sincere. It's tricky.

1. What is this monologue about?
2. Where are you? Describe wherever you are so that you are familiar with it. Maybe you are some place where you can't use your full voice? What happens when you do that?
3. Who are you talking to? Try talking to different people. A friend? A parent? A teacher? A grandparent? Maybe you're talking to a stranger on the bus?
4. What was your moment before? What happened just before you said these words?
5. What do you want? How are you going to get it?
6. What politicians share your views? Do *you* feel this way or not?
7. What do you know about elections? Are your parents politically active?
8. What do you know about global warming? If you choose this monologue, you should know what you are talking about.
9. How do you, the actor, feel about guns?
10. What do you mean when you say "it is selfless to vote?"
11. Are there any more questions that you can ask yourself?
12. Write an autobiography for this character. Build your character a life.
13. Remember the magic "if." What would *you* do if you were in this situation?

✒ **WRITE OUT** all of your answers. Be specific. It will get you closer to the truth of the scene, and you will create a stronger character.

⏳ **TIME YOURSELF.** This monologue was written to be about one minute long.

Divorce Boy or Girl

DRAMATIC

And so I'm supposed to do what? Just accept it? That would work out really well for you, wouldn't it? If I just made it simple. (Sarcastic) Oh, it's all good mom! (Pause) So, you'll just leave? Leave the house, the car, us? That's what you… (Off her reaction) DON'T SAY ANYTHING! You wanted to hear what I have to say, now I'm going to say it! (Pause) I am trying really hard not to hate you, mom. Really hard! You are ruining everything we have ever had. Look at dad. You have turned dad into a, a (Pause) And Violet? What about Violet? What's she going to do here without you? (Pause) Or do you plan on taking her with you? (Long pause. Off her look) Oh. You plan on taking her with you. Of course. She's always been your favorite. You can't live without her as much as she can't live without you. (Pause) So take her. Who cares? Who cares about anything? (Looking around) Look at this place. It feels like we never lived here.

CHALLENGE: This is a very emotional piece and requires you to find that emotional place before you even begin speaking. There are a lot of pauses. This character is emotional and thoughtful, meaning the character's rage is kept inside, but it is ready to slip out, as it does in the line, "DON'T SAY ANYTHING!" This character is deeply hurt. If you can't imagine a scenario this painful, then pass on this one. If you can, go for it!

1. What is this monologue about?
2. Where are you? This is your environment (smell, feel, see, hear). Be very specific. When you look around, what do you see? Describe the room you are in.
3. Who are you talking to? Obviously you are talking to your mother in this piece. What is she like? What emotional state is she in?
4. What was your moment before? What happened just before you began speaking? It appears she was talking to you. What was she saying? Write it out. Be specific.
5. You say your father has changed because of the impending divorce. How has he changed? Be specific. Write about his anger and pain.
6. Why is your mother leaving? What reasons did she give? Another man? Depressed?
7. Describe Violet. How old is she? Have you thought about life without her if she leaves with your mother?
8. You say that she has ruined everything you ever had. What do you mean?
9. What do you mean when you say, "I feel like I never lived here?" What are you going through when you say that?
10. Think of a situation where you have to tell your best friend that your mother is leaving. Write about it.
11. Are there any more questions that you can ask yourself?
12. Write an autobiography for this character. Build your character a life.
13. Remember the magic "if." What would *you* do if you were in this situation?

🖊 **WRITE OUT** all of your answers. Be specific. It will get you closer to the truth of the scene, and you will create a stronger character.

⏳ **TIME YOURSELF.** This monologue was written to be about one minute long.

DRAMATIC

Therapy   Boy or Girl

I told her I'm not going. She can ask two hundred times. She can chase me to the outer edge of the universe. I am not going to therapy. I don't need therapy. There isn't anything wrong with me. THERE IS NOTHING WRONG WITH ME! Okay, my room is messy. I admit it. What is the big deal? It's my room! I'm the one who is in there most of the time. I'd come out more if she would just… just cut me some slack. She doesn't like anything I do! Or anything I say. Or how I say it, for that matter! Or anyone I hang out with. All she ever does is find something wrong with my friends. I can't do anything with anyone without twenty questions. It's like I can't make a single decision without the ugly faces and the… look. You guys give me no credit. Even you! You don't know anything about me! All you know about me is what mom has told you and mom is a… You can tell her that if she takes me to therapy, I will leave and I will never, ever come back here. I mean it!

CHALLENGE: To not make it all one note. This is obviously a passionate piece. You will be tempted to speed through it. Recognize where there is a shift in the thought, and slow down or speed up. Did you just hear your mother's plan for you? Or did you hear it this morning and it has been festering? It will change the way you do this monologue.

1. What is this monologue about?
2. Where are you?
3. Who are you talking to? A school counselor? Your father? An older sibling? Maybe a grandparent that is staying at your house? This is a very important question.
4. What was your moment before?
5. What do you want? How are you going to get it?
6. Describe your messy room. Why is it so messy?
7. In your mind, what would therapy be like? Why are you so opposed to it?
8. Describe the ugly faces and the look. Make them real.
9. Where would you go if you left? Think about it. Are you serious or just threatening?
10. Describe the friends your mother does not approve of? Why does she act like she does about your friends?
11. Are there any more questions that you can ask yourself?
12. Write an autobiography for this character. Build your character a life.
13. Remember the magic "if." What would *you* do if you were in this situation?

✏ **WRITE OUT** all of your answers. Be specific. It will get you closer to the truth of the scene, and you will create a stronger character.

⧗ **TIME YOURSELF.** This monologue was written to be about one minute long.

The Stone

Boy or Girl

DRAMATIC

I got this stone. It says "Believe" on it. My aunt got it for me because she said I wasn't focused enough, that if I didn't settle my thoughts and think things through, that it would be hard for me to be successful at anything. She said that without discipline, I will be my own worst enemy. It's scary to think of being your own worst enemy, isn't it? But that's what she said. (Pause) She told me I have a wonderful imagination and I will be fine if I can focus. I told her I didn't know how a little stone could keep me focus and she smiled and squeezed my hand around the stone. (Pause) She died last week, my aunt. She got sick and she was gone very quickly. My mom said it was a blessing. I guess. At her funeral I was kind of off by myself and I watched everybody come and go. They were like those fuzzy monsters on a belt that you knock down with a ball. You know, like at a fair? I just sat and watched and squeezed my stone... I wasn't sad, really. I just felt calm.

CHALLENGE: To keep the pace going. This monologue will make you want to go very slowly. Don't go too slowly. It is heartfelt and sad, but remember, you are not sad. You are safe because your aunt gave you something special that gives you strength and focus. You may want to have a stone with you for this monologue.

1. What is this monologue about?
2. Where are you?
3. Who are you talking to?
4. What was your moment before? What happened just before you began speaking?
5. What do you want? How are you going to get it?
6. Describe your aunt. Use lots of details. Is she short? Tall? Fashionable? Describe her hair, her face, her voice.
7. Describe a funeral that you have been to. If you haven't been to one, what do you think it would be like?
8. Where were you when your aunt gave you the stone? Describe it in detail.
9. Where do you keep the stone? Where do you leave it at your house?
10. Where were you when you heard about your aunt's death? Did you cry?
11. Are there any more questions that you can ask yourself?
12. Write an autobiography for this character. Build your character a life.
13. Remember the magic "if." What would *you* do if you were in this situation?

✎ **WRITE OUT** all of your answers. Be specific. It will get you closer to the truth of the scene, and you will create a stronger character.

⧗ **TIME YOURSELF.** This monologue was written to be about one minute long.

DRAMATIC

Who Cares? Boy or Girl

This isn't the first time I've been in trouble you know. Remember last time? You caught me coming back in the doors by the auditorium? Remember? You said to me, "Come on now, I have enough trouble with the bad people, I don't need trouble from the good ones." I told you I just needed to run home for a minute and you told me to shut up. You didn't give a... hoot about why I left. You didn't care. Well guess what? I don't care either. I don't care about you, I don't care about this school. I don't care about anything. (Pause) No, that's not true. I want to be honest with you here. I do care about something. You know what I do care about? I care about my dog. She loves me. No matter what kind of mood I'm in, no matter how I act, she is always there. Always. Not my mother. Not my father. Certainly not you. My dog. Just my dog. I can count on her. She is the only one in my life that I can count on.

CHALLENGE: You are standing up to an authority figure. You have to remain somewhat respectful, otherwise your audience will think you are a punk and not someone who needs help. You always want to keep in mind that the audience has to be able to relate to you. If you come across as a total jerk, and the audience doesn't know why, they won't be able to relate to you; therefore, don't treat this person like an equal. He or she is not your equal.

1. What is this monologue about?
2. Where are you? This is your environment (smell, feel, see, hear). Be very specific. When you look around, what do you see?
3. Who are you talking to? A principal? A counselor? A teacher? A hall monitor?
4. What was your moment before? What happened just before you began speaking? Did you just enter? From where? What happened?
5. What did you go home for last time you got caught? Raise the stakes for yourself. Make it a really important reason that needed your immediate attention. Were you punished?
6. Describe this character's home life. You do not feel loved. What is it like? Make it up.
7. Describe your dog. Describe your relationship. What do you do to show your dog you love her?
8. What kind of trouble have you been getting in? Are things spiraling out of control? Make up something good to show you are a kid who is not getting the supervision or the attention you need.
9. Do you, the actor, get in trouble in your own life? When was the last time? What was your punishment?
10. Describe your school, especially the area around the auditorium doors where you got caught last time. You must have run home. Describe the distance home and the path you took.
11. Are there any more questions that you can ask yourself?
12. Write an autobiography for this character. Build your character a life.
13. Remember the magic "if." What would you do if you were in this situation?

✎ **WRITE OUT** all of your answers. Be specific. It will get you closer to the truth of the scene, and you will create a stronger character.

⧗ **TIME YOURSELF.** This monologue was written to be about one minute long.

Laying Down the Law · Boy or Girl

DRAMATIC

(On Phone) My parents won't let me ... I did ask. I begged! They said no ... Because they're afraid that people will be drinking and they don't want me to have the car there. They don't want me to go at all, but I promised them I wouldn't do anything ... Because they don't want to be responsible for anyone. They said if I can get a ride there and I promise not to get in a car with anyone who has been drinking, that I could go ... I tried to get the car ... SHUT UP! You drive then! Oh that's right, you don't have your license yet because your parents are making you wait until you're seventeen! ... So stop blaming *my* parents! They have every right to be distrusting after what happened with Blake and Carrie ... Are you serious? ... They were drunk, Debbie! ... You know what, fine. I'll see if I can get a ride with Richard. I'm done ... I'm done talking to you ... Deb, I am hanging up ... Good. I hope you have a great time downtown with- (Debbie hangs up on you).

CHALLENGE: The phone. It is always tricky when you are on the phone, but if you fill in the blanks (the ellipsis) with the words from the person you are speaking with, in this case Debbie, you will be fine. Always make sure you take enough time to hear the words coming through the phone. Debbie is being unreasonable, so you have to feel the anxiousness as the tension rises.

1. What is this monologue about?
2. Where are you? This is your environment (smell, feel, see, hear). Be very specific. When you look around, what do you see? Are you home?
3. Who are you talking to? Obviously you are talking to Debbie, but what is she like? Describe her. How do you know her?
4. What was your moment before? What happened just before you began speaking? Did you just talk to your parents? Or did Debbie call you? Try it both ways and see the difference.
5. Write out the whole conversation with your parents. Where did the conversation take place? Were they reasonable? Was the talk calm or did it get heated?
6. What kind of car do they have that you drive? How many people can fit in it? Where was the last place you went with Debbie in the car?
7. What happened to Blake and Carrie? Be descriptive. How did whatever happened to them affect everyone else?
8. Where is it you want to go? Is it a party? What do you expect the party to be like? Why do you want to go?
9. Who is Richard? Describe him? Why wouldn't Debbie just ride with him as well?
10. Debbie says something about going downtown. What is going on downtown? Who would she go downtown with?
11. Are there any more questions that you can ask yourself?
12. Write an autobiography for this character. Build your character a life.
13. Remember the magic "if." What would *you* do if you were in this situation?

✏ **WRITE OUT** all of your answers. Be specific. It will get you closer to the truth of the scene, and you will create a stronger character.

⏳ **TIME YOURSELF.** This monologue was written to be about one minute long.

DRAMATIC

The Policewoman   Boy or Girl

The policeman asked me if I ever heard my father say anything about wanting to hurt people. I said no. No. My father never even spanked us. I told the policeman that. There was a lady policeman there, too. A policewoman. And she asked the other cop to leave so she could be alone with me. So he leaves and she. . . she came over and sat next to me and she put her hand on my leg. And she didn't say anything. Nothing. She just rubbed my leg really gently. I remember thinking I could breath. I felt like I couldn't breath before that, like I hadn't taken a breath since we heard what happened. She was so nice. I just felt so … I was so afraid to let her see my face, like… like I did something wrong. Like it was me who did it. Then I finally looked at her. And she had a tear coming right down here. Right down her cheek. (Pause) I just… I just lost it.

CHALLENGE: Your emotions. This is a very deep monologue. Obviously your father has done something horrible and he has left you behind. That would be a very painful thing to have to deal with. In choosing this piece, you must be ready and willing to go there. Start out normally, as though you are telling a story. Then you must feel the pain all over again as you talk about the policewoman's kindness. Her kindness let's your emotions out. Who you are talking to will make a big difference with this monologue. Try talking to different people (a friend, a doctor, a minister, a sibling, etc.). This is a tough one. Are you ready for it?

1. What is this monologue about?
2. Where are you? This is your environment (smell, feel, see, hear). Be very specific. When you look around, what do you see?
3. Who are you talking to?
4. What was your moment before? What happened just before you began speaking?
5. What is your objective? What do you want? What are you going to do to get it?
6. What did your father do? I know it is hard, but you must answer this question. Use details. Where is he now?
7. How do you feel about your father now? Have you forgiven him? Are you still mad? Sad?
8. Describe the policewoman. Use as many details as you can.
9. Why were you able to breath when the policewoman touched your leg? That change in the way you felt is a very important feeling in this monologue.
10. Describe how you heard the news about your father. Use details. Set the scene for yourself.
11. When you saw the tear on the policewoman's cheek, what did you think? Why did you lose it?
12. Are there any more questions that you can ask yourself?
13. Write an autobiography for this character. Build your character a life.
14. Remember the magic "if." What would *you* do if you were in this situation?

✐ **WRITE OUT** of your answers. Be specific. It will get you closer to the truth of the scene, and you will create a stronger character.

⏳ **TIME YOURSELF.** This monologue was written to be about one minute long.

The Crash   Boy or Girl

It was so scary. It was really loud. I mean, like, REALLY loud! I can't stop hearing it. Every time I hear a loud crash, even if it's my mom dropping a pan in the kitchen, I jump. It drives me crazy. And then I feel everything again. Just from a sound. I can feel my heart beating so hard and I stop listening to everything around me. I can only hear that crash. And I hear Anna scream. She screams, "Oh my God!" over and over, like, "Oh my God! Oh my God! Oh my God!" And we were like whipping, like on a ride, but it was so fast but, like we were in slow motion. Like someone just slowed everything down for a second. It was so scary, but it was so fast. And slow, too. Is that possible? Then… then it was quiet. I remember seeing a man run past the car on Anna's side and I could hear him talking. Then I realized there was no door at all. And Anna was like, Anna just wasn't there. She just wasn't in the car anymore and her door was completely gone. Like in one second.

CHALLENGE: Speed. You have to talk fast, but you have to make sure we follow you through all your images. Car crashes are frightening. Make us see it and hear it and believe you really went through one. Pick up speed, then slow-down in certain places. And remember, it is totally up to you to decide whether or not Anna is okay. Her condition will make a difference.

1. What is this monologue about?
2. Where are you? This is your environment (smell, feel, see, hear). Be very specific.
3. Who are you talking to?
4 What was your moment before? What happened just before you began speaking?
5. What do you want? How are you going to get it?
6. Have you ever been in a car accident? What has ever happened to you that really scared you? Can you feel your heart beat faster at the thought of it? Try.
7. Describe the accident in this monologue. Make a clear picture for yourself. What happened?
8. Who is Anna? Describe her. Is she okay now?
9. What happened right after the accident? Did the police come? An Ambulance? Who helped you? Think and fill in all the blanks. Take it from the crash all the way until you got home.
10. Where had you and Anna been before the accident? What were you wearing?
11. Are there any more questions that you can ask yourself?
12. Write an autobiography for this character. Build your character a life.
13. Remember the magic "if." What would you do if you were in this situation?

✏ **WRITE OUT** all of your answers. Be specific. It will get you closer to the truth of the scene, and you will create a stronger character.

⧖ **TIME YOURSELF.** This monologue was written to be about one minute long.

DRAMATIC

First Love   Girl

You don't have to do anything if you don't want to. (Pause) Jasmine. You don't have to. If he breaks up with you because you don't want to do something, then he isn't good for you anyway. He's awesome. I think Jalen is great. But not if Jalen is going to insist you do something that you aren't ready for. That's just selfish. You should be able to just do things when *you* are ready. Not him telling you that you should be ready. Of course he's ready. He's a guy. But he needs to respect you. Ty respects me. He isn't pushing me to do anything. And he certainly isn't threatening to break up with me or to hook up with someone else if I don't do stuff. You need to be happy and not feel pressured into ... into being someone you aren't. If he breaks up with you because of that, then he's a total jerk, Jas. And you, you'll still be who you want to be. Right? Just don't feel like that. (Pause) You want me to have a talk with him? I will?

CHALLENGE: You have to be brave to talk about this subject. You are talking to a friend about a very sensitive thing. You will want to come on really strong, but it is sensitive and your friend does not need to be badgered about this. You may be the only one who knows what she is going through, so treat your friend with tenderness and still get your very strong point-of-view across to her. It is a tricky road to navigate, but you know you are doing the right thing. Good luck!

1. What is this monologue about?
2. Where are you? This is your environment (smell, feel, see, hear). Be very specific. When you look around, what do you see? How can you make your environment add to this scene?
3. Who are you talking to? In this case it is Jasmine. Who is she? Describe your relationship fully.
4. What was your moment before? What happened just before you began speaking? How did this scene get set?
5 What do you want? How are you going to get it?
6. Who is Jalen? Do you like him? Describe their relationship from your perspective.
7. Describe Ty. How long have you been dating? What do you guys do for fun?
8. Have you or anyone you know been pressured like this? How did it get handled?
9. Would you really have a talk with Jalen? What would you say? Be specific. How is he going to react?
10. Who gave you this advice that you are giving Jasmine?
11. Are there any more questions that you can ask yourself?
12. Write an autobiography for this character. Build your character a life.
13. Remember the magic "if." What would *you* do if you were in this situation?

✐ **WRITE OUT** all of your answers. Be specific. It will get you closer to the truth of the scene, and you will create a stronger character.

⌛ **TIME YOURSELF.** This monologue was written to be about one minute long.

DRAMATIC

Grounded

Girl

I didn't lie to you! Not about Bryant at least. He was not with them, I swear. They came by at like 11:30 and Bryant was not with them. It was just Traci and Shawna and Boomer. Honestly. I know I'm in trouble. Whatever. I get it. Whatever you think you have to do. It totally sucks though, I will say that. Because I'm going to get grounded or whatever for going to such a lame party. I know I shouldn't have gone. I know. But you guys were already asleep and they texted me and I … I just, I messed up. I wasn't thinking. I had everything done, all my homework and everything. You wouldn't even have known if Traci hadn't hit that car. AND SHE WASN'T TEXTING! She wasn't, I swear. And Bryant (Pause) I'm not even sure we are together anymore. He can be such a jerk. He was supposed to meet … I mean, he ended up going somewhere with some girls from South. I am so pissed at him right now, and now I'm grounded. I don't care. Whatever.

CHALLENGE: Your argument. You are trying to convince your parents that you did not lie, but you also snuck out so you still broke their rules. You need to save face somehow, so you need to convince them that what they are accusing you of is untrue, regardless of whether or not you snuck out. You won't come out a winner, no matter what. There are lots of starts and stops, so stay with your punctuation. It's a tricky one..

1. What is this monologue about?
2. Where are you? This is your environment (smell, feel, see, hear). Be very specific. When you look around, what do you see? How can your environment add to this scene?
3. Who are you talking to? Most likely you are talking to your parents as it is someone who has the authority to ground you. Make sure you define and describe whoever you choose.
4. What was your moment before? What happened just before you began speaking? How did this scene get set?
5. What do you want? How are you going to get it?
6. Traci must have gotten in an accident. Describe what happened. Where were you sitting in the car? Have a clear image.
7. Describe the situation when your parents were notified that you were with her. How did they react?
8. Try the monologue a few different ways; are you angry, sad, sorry, rebellious, embarrassed? It is up to you. Don't get stuck doing it one way until you try out a few.
9. Describe how you snuck out. Use a lot of details. Did you have to climb down? Did you have to sneak past your parents' room?
10. Describe all of your friends that were in the car. Have a clear picture of each of them.
11. Describe your relationship with Bryant. Who are these girls he was with?
12. Are there any more questions that you can ask yourself?
13. Write an autobiography for this character. Build your character a life.
14. Remember the magic "if." What would *you* do if you were in this situation?

🖉 **WRITE OUT** all of your answers. Be specific. It will get you closer to the truth of the scene, and you will create a stronger character

⧗ **TIME YOURSELF.** This monologue was written to be about one minute long.

55

DRAMATIC

The Foster Home   Girl

I didn't mean any disrespect. I know that's hard to believe, but, (Pause) Mrs. Fields, Mr. Fields, Reyna, I am really sorry. I'm just (Pause) I tripped out when I heard you guys had gone to dinner without me. I just— and it's not like you didn't have every right. You are a family. You don't owe me anything. You have done so much for me already. For my brother and me. I ... (Pause) You know my dad is getting out of jail next week. You know that. He doesn't have permission to go near my mom. She has a restraining order against him. But, she had a restraining order against him before when he put her in the hospital. And I am terrified he won't stay away from us this time. He said he hates me too because I look just like her. (Long pause) But, no matter what, I shouldn't have broken the window. I've got no excuse. I'm just really confused and scared ... I will pay for the window. I promise I will.

CHALLENGE: This is an emotional piece. That means that while you're trying to keep your emotions in check, you change direction in your thoughts. You have ellipsis and pauses. Know the difference between the pauses. You also have a dash. That means you change your mind mid-thought. Make sure you can do that. Watch your time and make sure it is one minute in length. It's tough subject matter and a tough monologue. Good luck.

1. What is this monologue about?
2. Where are you? Are you in the foster home? Describe wherever you are so that you are familiar with it.
3. Who are you talking to? This is a foster family. Describe them clearly so we know who they are.
4. What was your moment before? What happened just before you said these words?
5. What do you want? How are you going to get it?
6. Why are you in foster care? What happened? Describe in detail what happened that led to this.
7. Describe the incident of you breaking the window. What happened?
8. Describe your mother. What were her injuries that led to her being in the hospital? Is she okay now? How often do you see her? Describe your relationship.
9. Describe your father. Is he violent? Were you always scared of him? How long has he been in prison?
10. What is your relationship with your foster sister? How does it work to have a foster sister? Describe the family dynamic. Put yourself there.
11. Are there any more questions that you can ask yourself?
12. Write an autobiography for this character. Build your character a life.
13. Remember the magic "if." What would you do if you were in this situation?

✐ **WRITE OUT** all of your answers. Be specific. It will get you closer to the truth of the scene, and you will create a stronger character.

⧖ **TIME YOURSELF.** This monologue was written to be about one minute long.

Peer Pressure

DRAMATIC

Girl

It will make me feel weird? (Wait) Oh, a *good* weird. Is good-weird good? What is good about intentionally feeling weird? I don't even know what that means. You told me that cigarettes make you feel weird, too. After I coughed for twenty minutes and drank water from the river to save my life, yeah I felt a little weird. And you still smoke, Beth Lynn, which is so ridiculous. They taste like crap, they burn your lungs, and they make you stink. Ryan even told you that you stink. Not to mention that 'weird' feeling made me want to throw up. And that was only a cigarette! Now you want me to try this? I don't … I can't. I don't want to! I don't want to feel weird. I don't understand weird. I'm weird already. And Trisha acts like a total jerk when she does it. I'm not saying you act like she does, but still. You can't guarantee how it's going to affect me. It must affect everyone differently because you don't act like Trisha. It must depend on if you're ready for it and I'm not, I don't think. I don't want to be weird … Do I?

CHALLENGE: You are conflicted. You want to, but you don't want to. Peer pressure is a very difficult problem to navigate. You don't want to look bad or look weak, but you are smart. You already got pressured into smoking a cigarette and that went badly, and now here you are again. Beth Lynn is a good friend making bad decisions. Are you in?

1. What is this monologue about?
2. Where are you? This is your environment (smell, feel, see, hear). Be very specific. When you look around, what do you see? How can you make your environment add to this scene?
3. Who are you talking to? In this monologue you are talking to Beth Lynn. Who is she? Define her in detail.
4. What was your moment before? What happened just before you began speaking? How did this scene get set?
5. What do you want? How are you going to get it?
6. What does Beth Lynn want you to try? What do you know about this drug? Why are you so afraid of it?
7. Describe the cigarette incident. Use a lot of description so we can see it.
8. Who is Trisha? How did she act when she did whatever you are talking about?
9. You are questioning whether or not you should do it. Why? Are you insecure and want to fit in? Are you cool? Remember, this is your character. Make her whatever sort of person you want.
10. Have you been peer-pressured into doing anything else? Describe it.
11. What is your relationship like with your parents? What would they do if you got caught doing whatever Beth Lynn is trying to get you to do?
12. Are there any more questions that you can ask yourself?
13. Write an autobiography for this character. Build your character a life.
14. Remember the magic "if." What would *you* do if you were in this situation?

✎ **WRITE OUT** all of your answers. Be specific. It will get you closer to the truth of the scene, and you will create a stronger character.

⧖ **TIME YOURSELF.** This monologue was written to be about one minute long.

DRAMATIC

Respect   Girl

No, I don't see it that way at all. I think you are totally wrong about this. Try this. Try putting the shoe on the other foot. You go over to Terri's house and she is sitting there with a bunch of guys. You know all the guys. They are all your so-called friends. "You have nothing to worry about." Yeah, right. Then when you walk in and, all at once, the guys say they were just leaving. How would that make you feel? Would you be suspicious? (Off his look) Oh bull! Why would she be entertaining a bunch of guys without you being there? And then, to make it worse, you lied to her and told her you weren't at home as she was driving past your house. Then you told her, "Oh, they were just in the neighborhood and wanted to see my new motocross bike." Yeah right. Bethany told Terri she didn't even see your motocross bike. Look, we all know you like Bethany. Terri knows it, too. She's not an idiot, so don't make her out to be one. She's my best friend. You made her suspicious and now you are holding that against her. If you want to break up with her, then break up with her. But don't do her like that. She deserves better.

CHALLENGE: You are painting a scene for your audience about something you weren't actually a part of. You have to be careful with your speed. If you go too fast, you will lose your audience. And you have to imitate someone's voice, in this case, the sarcastic voice of the person you are talking to. Have fun with it, but don't go too over-the-top. You are making a point, but you are not a jerk.

1. What is this monologue about?
2. Where are you? This is your environment (smell, feel, see, hear). Be very specific. When you look around, what do you see? Are you in a park? Did this guy come to your house?
3. Who are you talking to? Make this kid real to you. Find him in a magazine or use a real male friend of yours. What is your relationship? How did it begin? What is his name?
4. What was your moment before? What happened just before you began speaking? He must have just asked you, "You see what I'm saying?" or something like that. You enter in the middle of a conversation. Think carefully about what you were saying before the monologue began.
5. Describe Terri. Use a lot of details. Why is she your best friend? Describe her family life.
6. Describe how Terri told you about this. Was she crying? Sad? Angry? Confused?
7. Who is Bethany? Are these girls all friends of yours, too?
8. Who else was there with Bethany? Describe everyone you are referring to.
9. Does your character have a boyfriend? Do you, the actor? Do you demand to be treated with respect? How can you relate to this situation?
10. Are there any more questions that you can ask yourself?
11. Write an autobiography for this character. Build your character a life.
1.2 Remember the magic "if." What would you do if you were in this situation?

🖊 **WRITE OUT** all of your answers. Be specific. It will get you closer to the truth of the scene, and you will create a stronger character.

⏳ **TIME YOURSELF.** This monologue was written to be about one minute long.

Instant Message

Boy

DRAMATIC

It has nothing to do with how smart you are or how good you are at soccer or if you are the captain of the lacrosse team. You have no idea how ridiculous you sound when you say that! She doesn't like you because she likes Taylor. She likes Taylor. Why is that so hard to believe? He's cool. You can compare yourself all you want. Taylor doesn't play lacrosse. Taylor got a C- on that test you aced. Taylor lives on East Market. Who cares? Obviously, Sydney doesn't care, so stop thinking she's going to suddenly care about that. Oh, and no, I am not going to go ask her if she got your instant message. You can handle that yourself. (Pause) Maybe she did block you, dude. Who would want someone who refuses to take 'no' for an answer? You wouldn't, so why would she? I'd block someone who wouldn't leave me alone, too. And now you want to fight Taylor. Why? You don't even know him and he has never done anything to you. Just get over yourself already and leave everybody alone!

CHALLENGE: When we stand up to a friend, we walk a fine line between sounding overly passionate and not being taken seriously. It is hard to do, especially when that friend is really popular and has no idea what they really look like. As the actor, it is your job to convince us that you love your friend and what you are saying is for his own good. This is fast, but don't go too fast. You are passionate, but don't preach. Find times to slow down. Should be a good one once you get it.

1. What is this monologue about?
2. Where are you? This is your environment (smell, feel, see, hear). Be very specific. When you look around, what do you see?
3. Who are you talking to? Describe your friend completely. How long have you been friends? Do you sleep over his house? Is he your best friend?
4. What was your moment before? What happened just before you began speaking?
5. Describe Sydney. Have you had to relay messages to her before? How did that go?
6. Describe Taylor. What is it about him that makes him more appealing to Sydney than your friend?
7. Your friend mentioned East Market Street as though there is something wrong with it. Why did he say that? Tell us about East Market Street.
8. Tell us about a time when your friend beat someone up.
9. Your friend probably told you what his instant message said. What did it say?
10. You must go to a rather large school if your friend does not even know Taylor. Describe your school.
11. Are there any more questions that you can ask yourself?
12. Write an autobiography for this character. Build your character a life.
13. Remember the magic "if." What would *you* do if you were in this situation?

✎ **WRITE OUT** all of your answers. Be specific. It will get you closer to the truth of the scene, and you will create a stronger character.

⏳ **TIME YOURSELF.** This monologue was written to be about one minute long.

DRAMATIC

Wrestling   Boy

I just . . . I just want to quit. I can't stand it. Wrestling is so boring, dad. Practice is no fun. At all. We have to run, we have to climb the ropes, we have to do stairs. Right there is like three of my least favorite things in the world. Besides lifting weights, which we also do, by the way. But honestly, I would deal with all of that. Seriously. But it's the losing weight thing. I absolutely hate not being able to eat. It's stupid. I'm starving all the time! Food is all I think about all of wrestling season. Wear a rubber suit, spit in a cup, check my weight all day long. It seems foolish to me. (Pause) I know you love it. And I know you really want me to be great at it. But (Pause) I hate it, dad. I hate it. I hate practice, I hate the matches, I hate the losing-weight thing. I'm not going to be that kid ... for you. I can't. I'm sorry.

CHALLENGE: To let your dad down easy. You have made up your mind it seems, but you haven't discussed it with your father, who seems to be your biggest fan. So you must take his feelings into consideration, while still stating the facts plain and simply. It's delicate.

1. What is this monologue about?
2. Where are you?
3. Who are you talking to? You are talking to your father in this case. Describe him. Describe him at your wrestling matches.
4. What was your moment before? What happened just before you said these words?
5. What do you want? How are you going to get it?
6. What do you, the actor, know about wrestling? What do people like about it?
7. How long have you been wrestling? Did your father wrestle? Brothers?
8. Describe where you have to run, where you have to climb ropes, where you climb stairs, and where you lift weights. Have a clear picture for yourself so your images are easy to find.
9. What do you eat when you are in wrestling training? Think about having to watch your food intake and describe a day's worth of eating.
10. Are you a good wrestler? Is that what your dad really loves and why he doesn't want you to quit?
11. Are there any more questions that you can ask yourself?
12. Write an autobiography for this character. Build your character a life.
13. Remember the magic "if." What would *you* do if you were in this situation?

✐ **WRITE OUT** all of your answers. Be specific. It will get you closer to the truth of the scene, and you will create a stronger character.

⧖ **TIME YOURSELF.** This monologue was written to be about one minute long.

The First Punch Boy

I punched him. I admit it. But he punched me first. Right here. (Hold your jaw) I bit my tongue really badly. I didn't even know he was about to punch me. I didn't even know he was mad at me. He just comes up and calls me a pussy. I was about to say, "What's up with that?" and he just cracks me. He was swinging, too. That's what I remember. Then his friend Brian punched me in the back of the head. It didn't really hurt, but I knew I got hit. I turned around and he had this look on his face like he was terrified or something. He was screaming, "Stop! Stop! Just stop." So I got to my feet and I looked down at myself, at my shirt, and it was bloody. That was when I saw Zach. He was just lying there. I looked around and all those other kids were there. I never even saw them. I mean, I don't know where they even came from. Then someone said that Zach was really hurt. And I … I didn't say anything. I didn't know what to say. I didn't mean to hurt him so badly. But you can ask anybody. He hit me first.

CHALLENGE: To make us believe you cannot remember anything. People really can forget what happens when they get into a fight. You need to convince us that you experienced it. You know what happened in the beginning, but then there is a section that you can't recall. We need to believe you. And it is wordy. Talk clearly.

1. What is this monologue about?
2. Where are you? This is your environment (smell, feel, see, hear). Be very specific. When you look around, what do you see? In school? In the police station? Principal's office? Home? Describe it.
3. Who are you talking to? Try it with different people. A cop, a friend, a parent, a teacher?
4. What was your moment before? What happened just before you began speaking? Perhaps someone asked you, "Did you punch him?" What exactly happened just before?
5. Why was he mad at you? You can assume you know by now. Was it mistaken identity? Did you kiss his girlfriend? Did you pick on his friend? Come up with a good story.
6. Who was this guy Zach? What do you know about him? Is he a bully? Are you?
7. Who is Brian. What did you see when you turned around and saw him? Do you know him?
8. Describe exactly where this fight took place. See it clearly in your mind. Have you been in fights before? Was this your first? Have you, the actor, been in a fight? Describe it.
9. Describe exactly what you saw when you saw all the blood and then saw Zach lying there. What happened exactly?
10. Are there any more questions that you can ask yourself?
11. Write an autobiography for this character. Build your character a life.
12. Remember the magic "if." What would *you* do if you were in this situation?

✐ **WRITE OUT** all of your answers. Be specific. It will get you closer to the truth of the scene, and you will create a stronger character.

⧗ **TIME YOURSELF.** This monologue was written to be about one minute long.

DRAMATIC

Bully

Boy

I told you. Right? I told you that things would go bad for you if I caught you here. Remember that? You were all tough, remember? "Hey, trailer trash!" Right? "Hey dumpster- diver!" You remember that? You and your friend Elton. "Take a shower, dirtbag! Ha, ha, ha!" That was you, right? I wanna be sure because ... because, I'm stupid. I'm a "scumtard!" Was that it? Scumtard? So, where is your friend now? I only see you and me. Nobody else. I saw you try to get across here as fast as you could. You were runnin' like a chicken-ass. But, hey. Sucks for you. Know why? Because you didn't make it across. And now, thanks to your big mouth and because your friend ain't here ... (Laughs) You're gonna cry now? You still cry? (Laughs harder) But you were so tough last week. Now you're cryin'? I bet your pants are wet too, right? Your friend Elton know? He know you piss yourself?

CHALLENGE: To be intimidating and mean, but calculating. You see, bullies are bullies because they are hurting. They are usually bullied themselves and so that is what they know. In this case, this kid picked on you when he had you outnumbered, but you had probably already picked on him. What are you going to do about it? Playing a tough guy is always appealing, but it can be a difficult undertaking. Don't play it too tough. You won't seem real. Give it a try.

1. What is this monologue about?
2. Where are you? This is your environment (smell, feel, see, hear). Be very specific. When you look around, what do you see?
3. Who are you talking to?
4. What was your moment before? What happened just before you began speaking?
5. What do you want? How are you going to get it?
6. Describe the kid you are picking on. Use as many details as possible.
7. Describe his friend Elton. He should be a bit intimidating to you.
8. Who bullies you? Describe the person. Give details about how he or she bullies you.
9. Do you bully others to? Where? When?
10. Think about this: How does it make you feel to bully someone? Powerful? Cool? Who do you brag to when you have scared someone or beat someone up? Anybody?
11. Do you get in trouble often? How do your parents react when you get in trouble?
12. Are there any more questions that you can ask yourself?
13. Write an autobiography for this character. Build your character a life.
14. Remember the magic "if." What would you do if you were in this situation?

✐ **WRITE OUT** all of your answers. Be specific. It will get you closer to the truth of the scene, and you will create a stronger character.

⧗ **TIME YOURSELF.** This monologue was written to be about one minute long.

A Bad Idea

Boy

DRAMATIC

I'm not doing it. I thought about it all night and I'm, I'm not going. If you guys want to do it, then do it. I won't say anything. But I'm too…I can't do it. You guys don't, I mean, your parents are…You don't have a father like mine. My dad would kill me. He would literally kill me! Like "in the ground" kind of kill me. You guys don't know him. He snaps. He punched my mother right in the face once. He did! He was so pissed. I thought he was going to kill her. My sister started crying or I think he would have. But he told me if I ever get in trouble that he would kill me. "I will take you out, you little punk." That's what he said. I know you guys can't picture it because you haven't seen him drunk. Well you have, Troy, but not these guys. Tell them. Tell them what he's like. So you guys just go ahead. I won't say anything. And you can use our wire cutters. Just bring them back. That's all I need is my father to find them missing. You can take them though. Just, Just leave me out of it.

CHALLENGE: This is a tough situation. Don't play it like you are weak, but rather scared. If these guys thought you were weak, they never would have asked you to join them in the first place. Be convincing that you truly thought about it, but thought better of it. Create a very strong situation for yourself. It will serve you well if you raise the stakes.

1. What is this monologue about?
2. Where are you? This is your environment (smell, feel, see, hear). Be very specific. When you look around, what do you see? How can you make your environment add to this scene?
3. Who are you talking to? There is somebody named Troy there. Who is Troy? Who else is there? Be specific. Give them all names and faces and build relationships with them.
4. What was your moment before? What happened just before you began speaking? How did this scene get set?
5. What do you want? How are you going to get it?
6. What is it you guys are talking about doing? Be very specific. If you are talking about doing something bad, have you thought about the consequences beyond your father's punishment? You thought about this all night. Have a clear picture of what you are refusing to do.
7. Describe the night your father punched your mother. What happened? Be specific.
8. Describe your sister. How old is she? Is your father abusive to her, too?
9. What does your father drink? Has his drinking ever gotten him in trouble With the law?
10. Describe the time that Troy saw your father drunk.
11. What happened the time your father warned you that he would "take you out?"
12. Are there any more questions that you can ask yourself?
13. Write an autobiography for this character. Build your character a life.
14. Remember the magic "if ": What would *you* do if you were in this situation?

✎ **WRITE OUT** all of your answers. Be specific. It will get you closer to the truth of the scene, and you will create a stronger character.

⧗ **TIME YOURSELF.** This monologue was written to be about one minute long.

Notes & Thoughts

Made in the USA
Middletown, DE
13 May 2022